REAL ESTATE
SUCCESS
SECRETS

Stories of Challenge, Triumph, And What It Takes To Build a Thriving Real Estate Business

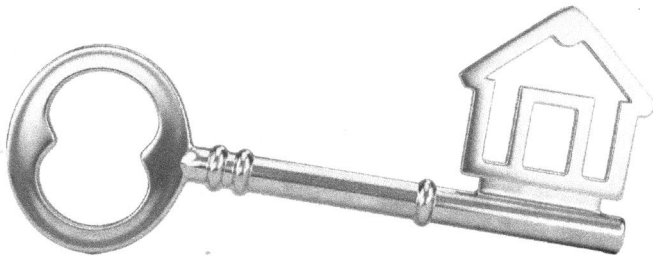

JESSICA HASTINGS-LESPERANCE

ADAM LESPERANCE | ALEXA MILLER | COLIN CAMPBELL | JENNA DAVIS
JENNIFER JONES | JENNIFER SILBERNAGEL | LIANNE TIMBERS-SHARP
MELISSA TAYLOR | RENATA PLECITY | SAM ABDALLAH | TERRI HASTINGS
TINA KOTHARI

Art Direction including Book Cover, Typesetting, and Layout Design Copyright © 2024 LeadHer Publishing

ISBN Ebook - 978-1-998411-02-3

For more information on the publisher LeadHer Publishing, visit www.leadherpublishing.com, www.instagram.com/leadherpublishing, www.youtube.com/@leadherpublishing or www.tiktok.com/@leadherpublishing

For more information on the Lead Author Jessica Hastings-Lesperance, visit www.instagram.com/realtors_resource or www.instagram.com/jess.hastings.l.real.estate

INTRODUCTION

I am thrilled to present to you a unique collaborative work, a compilation of narratives from Realtors® who have weathered the storms and basked in the sunshine of this dynamic industry. This book is not just a collection of stories; it's a beacon for anyone considering a career in real estate, or for those already navigating its waters.

In these pages, you will find an honest portrayal of the real estate world, and how each agent has found themselves not only inside the career but has found success within it – far removed from the often-perceived glamour and ease. It's a world where rainbows and sunshine are only part of the story, and the real essence lies in the grit and resilience that it takes to succeed. Through the experiences shared by various Realtors®, this book aims to illuminate the multifaceted nature of our profession — highlighting not only our triumphs but also the challenges and obstacles we overcome.

For those contemplating a career in real estate, these stories offer invaluable insights and lessons. You'll learn that success in this field is not just about closing deals and earning commissions; it's about building relationships, adapting to constant changes, and staying true to your values in the face of adversity.

But this book is not solely for Realtors®. It's also for our clients, the people who trust us to help them find their dream homes or sell their cherished properties. By sharing our stories, we hope to give you a glimpse into who we are beyond the business suits and open houses — the human side of the Realtors® you work with.

In essence, this book is a celebration of real life in real estate. It's about the journey, the learning, the unyielding spirit, and the heart that each Realtor® brings to this profession. Join us as we unfold the layers of our experiences, sharing the highs and lows that have shaped us into the professionals we are today.

Welcome to our world — a world where every day is a new chapter, every challenge a lesson, and every success a story worth telling.

Lead Author, Jessica Hastings-Lesperance

66

SUCCESS IN REAL ESTATE COMES NOT FROM WHAT YOU DO OCCASIONALLY, BUT FROM WHAT YOU DO CONSISTENTLY.

CONRAD HILTON

once. I came home one day, put my hands up, and yelled, "Sell them all, I am DONE!" I was done with being over-whelmed, being overworked, operating on next to no sleep, desperately craving more quality time with my kids, and wanting more financial security for my family.

This was the first time that my husband and I seriously considered real estate as a career. Being 'Raised with Real Estate'™, I had already been prospected for the career a couple of times. By growing up with a top market producer as your mom, you get a real front-row seat to what the actual life of a Realtor® looks like, and I knew I wouldn't be ready for it until now.

We planned to sell our other businesses and start a busi-ness in real estate. So, we listed everything for sale and started studying for our courses. We planned to get my husband licensed as a Realtor® first, and then I could prepare to get my license. As a wife and mother, I felt that I also had a duty to contribute financially to the family, as I had done with previous businesses, and to be ready for a new opportunity when all of our other businesses sold.

So, we each started studying for and writing our exams, one by one. We had a newborn baby on top of that and I was not getting any sleep. I didn't let that stop me. My husband and I would drive down to the exam centre and we would leave at crazy early times in the morning. I was rolling on about two hours of sleep and would write my exam, probably having studied three hours total, which was all I could fit in at the time. I failed the first exam I ever wrote, but not by much!

At this point, you were only given one attempt to pass the exam, and if you did not pass you had to pay for the entire course all over again. I remember calling the exam centre and the lady on the phone saying to me, "I don't think you're ready." I was devastated, but I knew deep down that she was right. I was tired, worn out, and needed some time to grieve my dad's passing, and so I did. I accepted the fact that I failed the exam, was glad to take some personal time for myself and my family, and more importantly, I stopped over thinking that I wasn't contributing financially – because I still was! I was caring for our household, taking care of our three children, and myself. For once, I could take a breath and just enjoy life.

It took a year to sell all of our businesses. My husband received his Realtor® license in five months, and we moved into our newly built house shortly after that. I remember sitting on our couch in our new house, holding my new baby after my husband had just gotten his real estate license…then the pandemic hit and we were suddenly in a lockdown.

So our family had just moved into our new house, and we had just sold off all of our businesses, then all of a sudden we couldn't go anywhere or do anything. I looked at my husband and said, "We will figure it out, let's get to work." Well, it turned out that real estate was an essential business during the pandemic – and it was a very hot market! You're probably thinking, "What a risky move," and you would be right, but with high risks come high rewards. We had no backup plan, so we knew we had to get our real estate business up and running. It was our only option. My husband started selling houses, and I started managing and growing the back end of his business.

The first year of our business was probably the most stressed I have ever felt. Having three kids and one income with an important, demanding business requires an immense amount of focus, especially since buying a home is arguably one of the most important purchases in someone's life. We found it difficult to manage our kids and manage our business at the same time. For me personally, I need to get my fitness and movement in every single day. I am a fitness instructor as well, and even on the days I don't teach, I still need movement to decrease my stress and ground myself.

To balance out our days, my husband would come home at midday so that I could practice my self-care and get my workout in. It became stressful when he wasn't able to leave work midday anymore because our business was booming and he was too busy with clients. Of course, this is a good problem to have, but I was frustrated and we both agreed that something needed to change.

Not long after this, I met someone in my yoga class who was looking for employment. I thought to myself, "This is perfect! Someone to help around the house and business is just what we need so we are both able to work and practice self-care!" So we hired her. She was our first house and business assistant – and having that help was a game changer! We went from being stressed out to being able to use our time efficiently and effectively. We were able to be better spouses for each other, offer better service to our clients, practice our self-care, and spend more one-on-one time with our children.

As we settled into this new and improved routine, I was finally able to study for my Real Estate license again. I was super excited that I was passing all of my exams, and then the lockdown struck again and our children were now online learning at home. Living in the country with very slow internet and everyone in the household trying to use it at the same time did not go over well.

Studying for my exams became impossible, and it started taking me longer to finish my courses. If you know me well, you know that once I put my energy and time into a task, I want to get that task completed as soon as possible. This long drawn-out process was tiring, slow, and felt extremely hard for me to do. I had maybe thirty minutes a day to study while everyone was at home. There came a point when I just had to accept the fact that my courses were going to take me longer to complete than what I had originally planned.

Eventually, the kids went back to in-person learning at school, and I was finally able to start really studying again. Things were going relatively well until I received my last final exam results. I failed the exam by 1%. Yep, 1%, you read that right. All of that hard work, time, and energy just to fail my final exam by one percent. So, I began studying once again and *finally* passed the entire course with time to spare!

I was looking forward to finally being able to do what I love, which is marketing and working on the big picture of our business. Coincidently, at this time, my husband and I were offered an opportunity to purchase the real estate business we were a part of. This was also the same business that my mother started from scratch and grew into the #1 team in our brokerage and board, and the #4 top-producing team in all of Canada for Keller Williams Group.

To say we were honored to be trusted with such a large undertaking would be an understatement. If you know my mother, this business is her life and for her to trust someone else with the business she poured her sweat, blood, and tears into is a huge deal. If my husband and I didn't possess the necessary skills to successfully operate the business, she wouldn't have offered us this opportunity, regardless of the personal relationship we have with her. One of the things she is best at is separating family from business, and just because I am her daughter and my husband is her son-in-law does not mean that we get any special privileges. In fact, during the first year of our real estate business, we received fewer leads and less help than other Realtors® on our team. There were times when this was frustrating, of course, but we now understand it was important that we were able to show her that we can operate a successful business without any special privileges or advantages. She wanted to know that she could trust us with her business and a growing team of Realtors®. We did eventually figure it out, and we are extremely grateful for the opportunity to grow an organic business of our own.

My entrepreneurship journey has been anything but easy. Juggling several successful businesses while being a young mom and trying to study was extremely difficult. Add in a family tragedy and global pandemic and you've got one overwhelmed entrepreneur on your hands. However, I got through it and it has shaped me into the formidable and successful entrepreneur I am today.

Fast-forward to today, we are coming up on our first anniversary of being co-owners of a 7-figure real estate business, leading an extremely talented team of Realtors®. That's not to say there haven't been many lows in our first year, because there have, but there have also been many highs. Both my husband and I are working on bringing the business to scale by working *on* the business, not in it. This is easier said than done as you can imagine. It has taken me almost a year to set up duplicatable systems for our team which has really pulled me away from actually selling homes. I find this hard sometimes because I'm often stuck feeling like I am torn between the two – selling homes and building up our business. However, I know that scaling our business is very important and if we don't have a solid foundation laid then there is no business to scale. We must have our systems clearly set out and ready to go. Luckily, this is what we had planned for. My husband is the rainmaker, while I am building the systems and our vision. Our vision with this business is BIG and I am super excited to execute it.

I have experienced a lot of success in my journey. Being Raised with Real Estate™ allowed me to learn from some of the best in the business. I chose to dive in, and my eagerness helped me discover my passion for this business. I'd say two of my biggest successes were getting my real estate license while having three kids in tow, and using my marketing strategy skills to help my husband's real estate business reach the top producer level in his very first year.

Another one of my successes was overcoming the expectation that I needed to jump right into selling real estate when I first obtained my license. And although I couldn't wait to start selling real estate, I knew this business would be different from the others we had owned before. For me, this business needed to be nurtured and carefully marketed so that it was ready to be scaled. After owning four previous businesses and growing up with real estate, I understood what roles my husband and I would each play in our first year.

One of the most important lessons I've learned was to overcome the expectations of others. Regardless of what profession my parent is in, I'm still responsible for my success. Every decision I have made to get myself here was still *my* decision. Taking advantage of an opportunity, a lead, or a mentor is simply a gift that does NOT guarantee your success; **it's how you use it that determines your success.** I had to do the work on my own, take the necessary steps to get myself here, make sacrifices, and really want it. When you carry on the family legacy, some onlookers like to undermine your character because of that. For me, I just wanted it. Being an entrepreneur just feels right to me; it's a passion for me.

I know my many failures – in addition to my successes – got me to where I am today, as they have shaped my professional career. I've created my own brand and owned this experience. I've had to work hard to create my own path. It's also been super beneficial having a coach who teaches me how to work on my mindset. I practice and work on my mindset A LOT.

A recommendation I have for any Realtor® is to overcome the common misunderstanding that you will only be successful if you have inside help. It's all about your mindset, and you can be successful without having a leg up. It's about each individual person and what you choose to do with your opportunities in life. It's about paving your own way, not whether or not you receive handouts. My parents had nothing when they built their real estate empire. Success comes to people who want it, just like I wanted it. It's about motivation. Success comes from inside of us; it's a desire and inspiration. There are all kinds of opportunities. We must take what we want and not be afraid to do that.

We need to trust in ourselves and be our own biggest cheerleaders because there will be times in our business when no one else is cheering for us along the way – and that is okay. This helps teach us the value of who we are and what we can accomplish. I believe anything is possible, but what we choose to focus on will help us to reach those goals. Always work on your mindset as your brain is a bunch of neurons ready to grow. Grow it by reading, listening to podcasts, attending webinars and seminars, coaching, networking, and working on yourself. Grow your mindset so big that no matter what you experience, you know it will all turn out okay, even if you don't succeed right away. Choose fear as your friend, constantly push your own boundaries, and remember that the sky's the limit!

Go out and get exactly what you want – and more.

KEY takeaway: Transform setbacks into the very foundation of your success, recognizing that the greatest achievements are forged through the fire of perseverance against failure. Stand firm, draw lessons from every trial, and carve a path to triumph with unwavering determination.

For more on Jessica Hastings-Lesperance:

www.instagram.com/jess.hastings.l.real.estate

www.instagram.com/raised.with.real.estate

www.jessicahastingslesperance.ca

www.facebook.com/raised.with.real.estate

or contact soldingreybruce@gmail.com

"

EVERY NO BRINGS YOU ONE STEP CLOSER TO A YES. KEEP PUSHING FORWARD.

BRIAN BUFFINI

ADAM LESPERANCE

🌐 terrihastings.ca
📷 @adamlesperance.realestate
📘 Adam Lesperance KW

Adam is your ultimate Canadian guide to finding your dream home or cottage in Grey Bruce and the surrounding area! As a Broker and Team Leader at Keller Williams Realty Centres, The Terri Hastings Real Estate Group, designated Luxury Realtor®, and recipient of the International Millionaire Agent Club, Adam's success stems from his extensive marketing strategies and dedication to helping his clients reach their property goals.

Adam has a natural background in entrepreneurship, and prioritizes community involvement by supporting local businesses, boards and young entrepreneurs, participating in community events, and encouraging environmental initiatives. Adam's goal is to create a life by design for his children, while also helping his clients find their dream home along the way.

CHAPTER 2
ADAM LESPERANCE

MY JOURNEY: *From Sheep to Showings*

As I sit down to scribble my thoughts for this chapter, it's like taking a step back in a whirlwind. Planning to start from the beginning seemed like a good idea until I realized my life's been like running on a treadmill while juggling flaming torches – always busy and a bit risky. Think of a growing snowball, but instead of snow, it's packed with tasks and ideas. Let me share with you my successes, struggles, and recommendations to have a thriving real estate business.

I was born in Wiarton, Ontario, a place so charming that you might miss it if you blink twice. I grew up on a farm just outside of the tiny village of Park Head, Ontario. Now, Park Head is a bustling metropolis of, oh, about 30 houses, and back then, it boasted the "Park Head General Store." This store was the epicenter of excitement for a kid like me – a treasure trove of treats and a blockbuster of rented movies. It was also a hub for community gossip and tall tales. The elders would spin yarns about Park Head's glory days, a time when it apparently had not one, but two stores, hotels, a train station, a flour mill, and a wood mill. It was the "it" place, even bigger than Owen Sound, which is now a thriving metropolis of roughly 30,000 people. (I should probably double-check that number.)

One of my earliest and most vivid memories as a young'un was watching the last train chug past the tracks near my parents' farm. It was like witnessing the end of an era. Not long after, those tracks were ripped up, and now the former railway system has been transformed into a multi-use trail. It's become a lifeline for tourism in our area, which keeps growing like a teenager in a growth spurt.

The Bruce Peninsula, where we live, work, and play, is genuinely unique. It's dotted with several inland lakes and hugged by Lake Huron to the West and Georgian Bay to the East. Growing up here was an adventure every day, especially on our farm. It was mainly a Dairy, Beef, and Syrup farm, but my parents were always up for agricultural experiments. They dabbled in everything from garlic and bees to apples and, I suspect, alchemy. You never knew what you'd find in our barn!

Stepping into real estate in January 2020 was like jumping onto a moving train. Before this daring leap, my life was an eclectic mix of adventures. Selling "Woody's Arborist" – a tree removal business I started from scratch – wasn't just shedding a business; it felt like saying goodbye to old, leafy friends. Selling "Lamblicious" – a business my wife started from scratch as well – and closing the "Wiarton Fitness Centre" were other chapters in my saga. And let's not forget selling and returning the sheep flock to my parents, (when I was 16 I asked for sheep for my birthday, yes sheep) it's not every day you get to say, "Here, have some sheep!" All this while we built a new house in just five months, because who needs sleep, right? Our three kids, Nash, Arkelle, and Kolby, were joining the same school I terrorized – I mean, attended – as a kid, adding to the excitement.

Dreaming of being a Realtor® since my younger days, I always thought it'd be cool, like being a detective but for houses. We had already flipped a couple of properties, built a cottage, and turned our old home into a duplex, proving that yes, I can indeed use a hammer without smashing my thumb.

My real estate journey was partly nudged along by my mother-in-law, who started her business around the same time that I started the tree business. Our early days in the new businesses were like those awkward first dances at school – stepping on toes but eventually finding the rhythm.

Then something happened. We needed a short-term loan for the flips. Terri to the rescue! *"Hmm,"* I thought, *"this real estate stuff is likely more lucrative than the tree cutting, and seems to have far less risk of falling out of a tree."*

My first chat with Terri about joining real estate was memorable. She doubted my fit for the role, but I've always loved a good *"watch-me-prove-you-wrong"* moment.

In the early days of my real estate adventures, I was greener than a freshly mowed lawn in spring! Dealing with my first clients and deals, I was as nervous as a cat in a room full of rocking chairs. There I was, checking, double-checking, and then triple-checking everything. I'd run to the experienced agents on the team for advice like a kid running to their parents after a nightmare. Their support? Absolutely stellar. It was like having a real estate Yoda at my disposal.

Slowly but surely, my confidence started to build up. It was like watching a skyscraper being constructed, one exhilarating floor at a time. Learning new things became my daily bread – and let me tell you, it's the tastiest bread ever. One of the coolest perks of this gig? Getting to soak in perspectives from a kaleidoscope of people. It's like attending the world's most interesting dinner party every day.

And the numbers! Oh, the numbers from the random assortment of businesses that come up for sale – they're like pieces of a puzzle waiting to be put together. And as Mike, the sage of our team, once told me: "Every deal is different." Truer words have never been spoken. Each deal is like a snowflake, unique and full of opportunities to learn and hone your skills. It's a never-ending rollercoaster of learning, and honestly, I wouldn't have it any other way.

In my grand tour of the real estate world, I've learned a few things. I've heard a common refrain from numerous folks who've dabbled in property investing: "I wish I never sold that house, triplex, etc..." It's like they all missed the same boat, or maybe they sold the boat too soon. So, here's my two cents: cling onto properties for the long haul. It's a lot easier to play the long game if your properties are actually making money, not just sitting there looking pretty. We all have those "the one that got away" properties. I'm still on the lookout for a time machine on eBay.

Buying property is a smart move. You put down a little and, historically, watch as it climbs up in value over time – like a financial "Jack and the Beanstalk." But here's a heads-up for the first-time investors: they're sometimes a tad too starry-eyed about the monthly "cash flow." Unless you've stumbled upon a hidden gem, you're probably just going to break even or get a small profit each month. Real estate investment isn't a get-rich-quick scheme; it's more like a "get-rich-eventually-if-you're-patient" kind of deal. Your tenants are basically your unofficial business partners, chipping away at your mortgage. And as tenants come and go, you get to hike up the rent a bit, which is always a nice bonus.

The market gets better, you refinance, pull out some equity, and voila – you're ready to buy again. It's like playing Monopoly in real life, except with less arguing over who gets to be the car and no one flipping the board in frustration.

Another golden nugget of advice: always have great tenants. It sounds like a no-brainer, but it's astounding how much of a difference it makes. We always end up with fantastic tenants, which I suspect is partly due to some positive mindset voodoo on our part. Keeping things upbeat and having open communication lines really does wonders. It turns the whole landlord-tenant relationship into less of a "nail-biting thriller" and more of a "buddy comedy."

The first year in real estate felt like playing a game where you don't know the rules. Balancing family and work was like trying to solve a Rubik's Cube in the dark. The paperwork alone was like a never-ending game of Whack-A-

Mole. My schedule was more tangled than headphones in my pocket, often leading to some comical double-booking situations. Eventually, we got some help with the kids, because cloning myself wasn't an option... yet.

The second year was a rollercoaster that only went up. Working with my coach, Jenifer, was like having a personal cheerleader, minus the pom-poms. We bought more properties, including a snazzy building in Wiarton and a whole island in Lake Huron – because who doesn't want their own island? This success made me ponder the true meaning of success. Was I just chasing my tail, or actually catching it?

Oh, the early days with Jenifer, when I faced The Great Phone Dilemma! In my tree removal days, my phone was like a hot potato – constantly ringing with people wanting quotes, wood chips, you name it. So, there I was, asking Jenifer, "How on Earth do you turn this thing on?" because, in real estate, phones don't magically ring by themselves. You have to be like a detective, searching for the calls.

Jenifer, wise as an owl, explained that real estate is a different beast – you need to chase the leads, not wait for them. This was the most challenging part for me. I'm an ace at answering calls, zippy with email replies, and a wizard with text responses. But hunting for leads? That was a new game.

So, I started dialling numbers like a telethon host. Call, call, and call again. And guess what? It worked! Plus, once you prove you're good at what you do, people actually start calling you. The catch in real estate is the whole "people-move-every-eight-years" thing. It's not like selling shoes where folks might come back for more every few months. You've got to get out there, be genuine, and really listen to people.

Here's the funny part: I've overheard so many people talking about buying or selling property. And there I am, too chicken to jump into the conversation. Then, a few weeks later, boom! Some other Realtor® wraps up a deal with them. If only I had a time machine, I'd zip back, give myself a pep talk, and dive into those conversations. Missed opportunities – the bane of every Realtor®'s existence!

Now, as a real estate broker and co-owner of THREG (Terri Hastings Real Estate Group), with a small army of four offices and 10 agents, life's a circus, and I'm always learning. My wife, Jessica, a Realtor® and our Operations Director is the superhero sidekick in this dynamic duo. We're the Batman and Robin of real estate (cape optional). I've adopted a healthier lifestyle, waking up at an hour even the sun finds ungodly, for meditation and exercise. Eating healthy is my new normal – kale and I are now on first-name terms.

My recommendation to other Realtors® is to focus on building real relationships, even if that means occasionally listening to long stories about someone's cat. I've learned the art of listening – it's amazing what you hear when you're not talking.

As for my advice, here are my top 15 ultimate recommendations:

-Wander through life, making connections that feel natural.

-Get to know everyone, and let them get to know you.

-Stay honest and kind; it's a timeless strategy.

-Enjoy people and things around you; life's too short for anything less.

-Treat life as a game; play it with enthusiasm and bold objectives.

-List-making is your secret weapon; it keeps chaos at bay.

-Being punctual is not just polite, it's powerful.

-Count and celebrate everything – people, places, moments.

-Approach things with a strategy, aiming for a grand finale.

-Cherish friendships, and stay true to your word.

-Embrace real-life interactions; they often mean more than digital ones.

-Remember, not everyone's online – some still use phone books!

-Build trust over a cup of tea; it's the best foundation.

-Allocate extra time for stories from the wise and retired; they're hidden gems.

-When you speak, are you listening? Listen often and when you speak, do it strategically.

Moving forward, I try to keep a smile on my face and a spring in my step. My motto is to stay positive and appreciate the present – it's a gift, that's why they call it the present, right? Being happy at work, quick to respond, and always ready to lend a hand are my guiding stars.

The secret to who you are and how you feel is like a secret recipe, and it's all in your head! Think of your mind as Play-Doh – squishy, mouldable, and ready for fun. Why not treat each day like you're the star player in the "Game of Life"? Strut around like you've just rolled a double six and landed on "Free Parking."

Here's the game plan: have a blast with life. Be the character you'd root for in a movie, the one with the catchy one-liners and the enviable wardrobe. When you do the right thing and help others reach their goals, you're not just earning brownie points; you're building trust and stepping up as the MVP in your life's team.

Living in the moment? Absolutely! But keep one eye on the horizon, like a pirate searching for treasure. Don't be scared to switch lanes or try a new hat. Maybe today you're a cowboy, and tomorrow, who knows? A space ranger?

Remember, time is like that last slice of pizza at a party – it's precious, and once it's gone, it's gone. So, choose wisely how you spend it. Do you binge-watch another reality show, or do you go out and make your own reality the best show ever? The choice, my friend, is yours!

In conclusion, my journey into real estate is not just about selling properties; it's about building a life that's as exciting as a mystery novel, as fulfilling as a five-star meal, and as rewarding as finding that lost TV remote. It's about creating a story worth telling, with a few laughs along the way.

KEY Takeaway: Remember, all those random skills and oddball experiences you've racked up over the years?

Turns out, they're not just party tricks! Whether you were a champion cheese roller, a master of medieval literature, or a wizard with a spreadsheet, those unique talents and life lessons are gold in your real estate career. And let's not forget the universal superpower: building relationships. It's like the Swiss Army knife of business skills — always useful, never out of style. So, go ahead, unleash your inner Renaissance person and watch your real estate career flourish with a mix of flair and friendliness!

For more on Adam Lesperance:

www.terrihastings.ca

www.instagram.com/adamlesperance.realestate

www.facebook.com/adamlesperancekw

"

EVERY NO BRINGS YOU ONE STEP CLOSER TO A YES. KEEP PUSHING FORWARD.

BRIAN BUFFINI

ALEXA MILLER

🌐 alexamillerrealestate.com
📷 @alexamillerrealestate

Alexa has been in real estate since 2016. She started as an executive assistant to her mentor before getting licensed in 2019.

Alexa is a designated Luxury Real Estate expert with Keller Williams Realty International and specializes in selling residential, waterfront, and farmland. She lives on the beautiful Bruce Peninsula with her husband Graham, daughter Harper and their two labs.

CHAPTER 3
ALEXA MILLER

"ORDER UP!" – A phrase I heard every few minutes at the restaurant I was working at full-time at the age of 21. Did I hate my job serving? No. But did I love it? Also no. I had just moved back home to Ontario from Alberta after spending a year partying, exploring the Canadian Rockies, and, quite frankly, trying to figure my life out. As soon as I got back to my hometown of Wiarton, I picked up my old serving job at a local Golf and Country Club. I did love the hustle and bustle, the people, and the money, but I hated the late nights and early mornings when I was scheduled to open and close the bar. At that point in my life, I was still a bit of a lost soul, without a clue as to where I was headed.

One night while at my serving job, my dad sent me a text: "Terri Hastings is hiring an assistant, you should apply." Terri was the queen of real estate in our entire area, and even if you didn't know her personally, you knew her name. At the time I wasn't thinking of getting another job but when he told me about the opportunity, I couldn't think of a reason not to go for it. I wanted to try something new, and this seemed like it could be a good fit. I applied for the job and before I knew it, I was hired, handing in my resignation at the restaurant, and switching my serving apron out for a fancy blouse and heels.

Terri was a force. She was intimidating at first, but I was fascinated by her strong personality and extreme confidence. When she walked into a room, you stopped to listen. I wanted to be her. I wanted people to look at me like that and see me as a successful woman in business. The first few days were overwhelming. I knew nothing about working in an office setting and I didn't know the first thing about real estate. I still remember being scared to answer the phone for a good week. I quickly realized that I was either going to sink or swim with this job, so I swam as hard as I could. Thankfully, after a few short weeks, I quickly caught on to the systems and daily tasks and started to fall in love with the position.

It wasn't long after I started working there that Terri approached me about getting my license to join alongside her in selling. I was more than ready and knew it was what I wanted. After about two years of working on the administrative side of things, I jumped into the courses and started studying. It wasn't easy; I was working full-time during the week which meant I had to pencil in my study time in the mornings, evenings, and weekends. Although I had experience in a real estate office, I failed two out of the five exams and had to retake them. I also lacked any confidence back then and cannot tell you how many times I would cancel and reschedule an exam because I was petrified I wouldn't pass. After a very long year and a half, I finally completed my last exam and was on my way to becoming a licensed Realtor®.

Although I was already a part of the team, I was so ecstatic to officially start selling real estate with the rest of my colleagues. I was ready and determined, and quite honestly, I hit the ground running. It was a whirlwind! Before I even had the official license in my hand, I got a call about a potential listing from a family member. The day I finally got the license in the mail I was allowed to start trading, and my team leader, Terri, set me up that night to show a house for the first time, all on my own. Lo and behold, the buyers fell in love with the property (which was a stunning waterfront property, by the way), and they bought it that night.

On my first official day of being a licensed Realtor®, I sold my first home. I think I smiled for a week straight. That deal came with some struggles and bumps in the road (as almost every deal does), but my mentor, Terri, supported me and helped me through it. Terri set me up for success – and for that, I will forever be grateful. The moral of this part of my story is to get a mentor and a team that will be an integral part of helping you succeed in this business.

Over the next year, I continued to work as an assistant to Terri while selling on the side. I did 13 deals and was more than thrilled with that. After that first year, we decided that I was getting busy enough with selling that it was time we hired a new administrative assistant so I could sell full-time. I was elated to be moving up in my career, but this couldn't have happened at a worse time. (Or so I thought.)

It was March 2020, and the world had just been shut down due to the COVID-19 pandemic. We were ordered to work from home, wear masks in public places, and social distance from our family and friends. I started to panic. How was I going to survive solely on commission sales when we weren't even allowed out of our houses? I figured the market was going to crash and I'd have to beg for my old job back so I could garner a bi-weekly paycheque again. Until then, I was ready to do whatever I had to do. I took the first bit of downtime to cultivate my systems, amp up my lead generation, and reach out to my database to see how everyone was doing during lockdown. Before I knew it, and much to my surprise, the real estate market became a force to be reckoned with.

I will take this opportunity to share that I am very lucky to live and work in cottage country, a beautiful area known as the "Bruce Peninsula" where we are surrounded by Georgian Bay and Lake Huron. We are located about three hours north of the GTA. When we learned that the lockdown wasn't going to end anytime soon, our phones would not stop ringing. People were calling us from all over Southern Ontario. Some were looking to buy a cottage so they wouldn't have to quarantine in the city, others needed to sell their condos and buy something bigger for their family, and many were selling their homes to buy lake houses due to their offices closing until further notice. Since real estate was considered an essential service, many rules and safety precautions were put in place and we were still allowed to meet with clients and show houses.

The real estate market took off. Homes were seeing multiple offers and selling way over asking due to pent-up demand and low-interest rates that were caused by the pandemic. For most sellers, the real estate market during COVID-19 was a "lottery market." I didn't have to ask for my old job back after all. Sometimes I look back and feel as though this time in my career was all a blur. This opened my eyes and made me realize that not even a global pandemic can stop the real estate market. No matter what is going on in the world, people still have various needs and will always be buying and selling. At this point, I don't even think a zombie apocalypse could shut it down.

This brings me to years two through five of my real estate career, closing many deals on both the listing side and buy-side and learning constantly along the way with the help of my mentor, team, and brokerage. Due to the area I trade in, most Realtors® in my market sell all types of real estate, including myself, however, I do have a "niche" market I like to work in. Two, to be exact. I will happily sell anything from raw land to a commercial building but my passion is selling waterfront and farmland. I will happily show property at 8:00 p.m. on a Saturday evening if it means getting the opportunity to view a luxurious Georgian Bay waterfront while watching the sunset, or if it means exploring a 100-acre farm with sprawling field views. My passion for waterfront properties comes naturally from growing up in our area, surrounded by endless lakes and bays, and being raised with a farming background has allowed me to specialize in selling farmland.

Finding a niche that you want to specialize in is no easy feat. It takes time and experience with all sorts of different buyers, sellers, and properties to determine what markets you thrive in and what brings out your passion. It will take a few years to learn what type of agent you are and want to be, whether that be both a listing and buying agent, or solely a listing or buying agent, or maybe an agent that works in one neighborhood only, versus the whole city. These things will also surely change throughout your career. Right now, I work with all sorts of clients, but my long-term goal is to be a listing agent only. This will eventually come with more time and experience in the business.

I have had many successes and struggles along the way, as any Realtor® or business owner will. From crushing my personal goals year over year to *almost* getting sued in my second month of being an agent, each obstacle and triumph along the way has made me a better person, real estate agent, and businesswoman. Each deal we close is a learning curve and we will never know everything, no matter how long we are in it, which is why it is so important to surround yourself with people who will always be there to support, guide, and cheer you on as you navigate your career. There are days that I cry and want to quit. There are days that I sit there, reflect, and cannot believe I got to where I am – and I am proud of myself. It won't always be easy, but it will be worth it.

Real estate was never originally in the cards for me. I didn't grow up with the dream of selling houses. I wanted to be a nurse, own a beauty salon, or be a horseback riding instructor, but when the opportunity was given to me it felt like the stars aligned. I had no idea if I would be a good real estate agent. I saw how hard my mentor worked, the hours she put in, and the crap she dealt with daily, and I still didn't shy away. I took a chance on myself and that's how I got to be where I am today. I don't make a million dollars a year – in fact, I don't make even close to that – but I continue to grow year over year and set new goals that will set up a life by design for myself and my family. Maybe one day I will make a million dollars, but until then, I am fully committed to continuously growing, learning, and following the road wherever it takes me. I have only been a real estate agent for five years. I have many years ahead of me to take what I can from the world's cookie jar. Maybe in 30 years, I will write another chapter in a book and you can read about where I ended up.

No matter what stage you are at in your career, don't forget to take the time to continuously invest in yourself and your business. It's easy to get caught up in the money, success, and "busyness" of this career, but at the end of the day, as my mentor, Terri Hastings, also says: "You're only as good as your last deal."

KEY takeaway: Being focused on consistent growth and evolution will serve you well in life and business. Don't be afraid to open a door that you didn't think was for you at first – you never know where it can lead!

For more on Alexa Miller:

www.alexamillerrealestate.com

www.instagram.com/alexamillerrealestate

www.facebook.com/alexamillerrealtor

COLIN CAMPBELL

🌐 campbellteam.ca
in ColinCampbell-KWRC
📷 @sircolin_campbell

Colin Campbell is a distinguished leader and accomplished entrepreneur in the Canadian real estate industry. As the COO, Broker & Owner of Keller Williams Realty Centres, Colin has cultivated a reputation for excellence, both in his own professional endeavours and in those of his agents. Colin's vision for the brokerage is to enable his agent partners to build fulfilling careers, create successful businesses, and generate wealth that will leave a legacy for themselves, their families, and their communities.

Through his commitment to helping his agents establish strong networks and build great teams, Colin has earned recognition internationally. He takes great pride in building an office of equality and inclusion. Colin is a respected voice in the real estate industry, and his insights and expertise have been sought after by top media outlets.

CHAPTER 4
COLIN CAMPBELL

"IT TOOK me 20 years to become an overnight success."
Kevin Hart's words resonate with me as I reflect on my
path from a newcomer to Canada to the owner of Keller
Williams Realty Centres, a thriving Real Estate brokerage
in Newmarket, Ontario. My career took years of learning,
filled with trials and triumphs before I gained any sense of
success.

It was 2001. I arrived in Canada as a new immigrant and
newlywed. Navigating an unfamiliar land was challenging. I had just stepped off of the plane and I already felt
like I was behind. Everything seemed so fast-paced. But
my goal to build a life for my family was as clear as day. I
had dreamt of this opportunity all my life, and now it was
here. I was going to be successful. I had no idea how – but
I knew it was going to happen one way or another.

I began my career the same as many others and the only
way I knew how: retail sales. I was 23 and for my first job,
I stood outside of subways and sold newspapers on
commission. With no Canadian experience, it was the

only job I was offered. I was willing to do whatever it took.

As challenging as it was, this job was a fundamental stepping stone to my career. It was here that I was able to apply the basics of sales. The most important of which was connecting with people. Most of the time I was ignored or cussed at. There was the odd occasion, however, when I had genuine interactions. I made them laugh and walk away feeling better about their day, and themselves. It was then that I learned something I could never find in a book. Authenticity. When you're genuine with others, they can feel it. When they leave with a smile on their face, they'll come back. The secret of sales is relating to people. When you understand that, you can sell anything. The important part is connection.

After that, I moved on to Radio Shack. I rose through the ranks from a part-time associate to a District Sales Manager position, and I gained a crucial base of knowledge for my career. Yet, I still felt something was missing. I moved from brand to brand selling different items, but I became tired of clocking in and working for someone else. During this time, I was fascinated by real estate. I had always wanted to move into this area, but I was afraid to take the leap. I had become comfortable in the safety of a regular paycheck and I had responsibilities to my family. In real estate, I knew I would wake up every day unemployed. But I knew if I worked for myself as hard as I did for everyone else, I couldn't fail.

A decade into my journey – with the help of my wife – I took a leap of faith into the realm of real estate. Dave Chappelle's wisdom echoed in my mind, "Success is not final, and failure is not fatal." Each step in my journey was a learning experience, preparing me for this new adventure. In the beginning, it was hard. I quit my job and became a full-time student. For six months I studied for eight hours a day. Once I had finally obtained my license, I realized I did not have a long list of contacts, because I wasn't from here. I had just begun and I already felt behind. I had only my friends and family, most of whom were immigrants as well.

I persevered anyway. My next step was to choose a brokerage. Choosing Keller Williams was a deliberate decision, as their unique culture of sharing expertise and resources was a perfect match for my vision. The brokerage has a reputation for providing a roadmap to their agents for building a successful real estate business. Keller Williams' spirit of collaboration and cooperation among agents aligned with my belief that success is not a solo endeavour. It's a collective effort. Moreover, Keller Williams had written the real estate Bible, *The Millionaire Real Estate Agent.*

At this point, I had studied for six months, gained my license, and had chosen a brokerage. People often think that once you get your license, money will fall from the sky and float gently into your pocket. That was not my fate. There is a Chinese proverb that states:

The growth of a Chinese bamboo tree is a patient process. It requires daily watering, fertilization, and nurturing. Remarkably, this tree remains hidden beneath the ground for five years. However, when it finally emerges, it rapidly ascends to a towering height of 90 feet in just five weeks.

And so, I went out every day, rain or shine (literally), to door-knock. I had practiced with my children, making them stand by the door while I gave them my pitch. Every day for nine months, I went out. And every day for nine months, I came home with no results. By this time, we had run through our savings and were operating in the red. We were going to the food bank with our young children to make ends meet. It was the lowest point of my life.

But I had been learning my craft. Learning to be relentless, to dig deep. At this point, failure was not an option. Giving up was not an option. I had to double down. You will never know how strong you are until being strong is your only option. I knew more contacts meant more contracts, so I found a cold-calling system. I door-knocked every morning and cold-called every afternoon.

At the same time, I attended every training my office held. I was the first to show up and the last to leave – literally turning on and off the lights for the building. I made myself visible, I found mentors and shadowed them. I surrounded myself with people who inspired me. They allowed me to protect my mindset. I saw it being done so I knew it was possible. In the words of Jim Rohn, "You are the average of the five people you spend the most time with." So I became a mosaic of my inspirations.

After some time, my efforts began to pay off and contracts started coming. My children would come home from elementary school and tell me how their friends had my magnets on their fridges. I was happy to be putting food on the table, but I was still hungry for more. I had now been working at Keller Williams for eight years, so I sought out the owner and asked him if he would be my mentor.

I made sure to put myself in a circle of people on an ownership path. We met regularly, challenged each other, and pushed each other. I invested in a real estate coach who was willing to get me to the next level. Today, we have access to anyone we want to learn from. Google is your best friend, or in my case, Audible. I became a voracious listener of audiobooks by great business people. One life hack to remember – **anything you want to do, someone has done it before. So seek them out and learn from them.**

While I worked as an agent, I was preparing for the next step: ownership. When the opportunity presented itself, I was ready for the challenge. New opportunities will always be knocking at your door, you just have to be ready to invite them inside.

I think sometimes life will test us to see how committed we really are to achieving our goals. So, when at work, trust the process. Like the bamboo tree – plant, water, tend. There is a proven system that works. Listen and learn from those who have come before, the agents who are where you want to be. Trying to jump ahead means you will miss crucial elements along the way. **Shortcuts will get you lost. You can't cheat success. You have to create a habit and play the long game.** Water the plant every day; small consistent steps are better than no steps. Motivation and discipline are fundamental tools for success. You may have motivation now, but I promise you, there are days when that will wane. Discipline won't. That's when routine shifts into gear.

The principle of compound effect is a powerful guiding force. By consistently door-knocking/cold-calling, learning from my so-called failures, nurturing relationships, and making strategic alignments, my real estate business began to thrive and grow exponentially over time. It's the daily, consistent efforts that, when compounded, lead to lasting success.

When I think back to the time that I ran my first half marathon, the memories are still fresh. I was new to long-distance running, having trained for six months leading up to the race. As I got halfway into the race, my time was on point, and everything seemed to be going according to plan. However, my competitive spirit was soon tested. A man, despite having a disability in one leg, swiftly over-took me. My pride took a blow. But the universe seemed to have more humbling lessons for me, as shortly after, a woman, who appeared to be in her early 70s, breezed past me too.

The competitor in me couldn't resist. I tried to catch up, increasing my pace significantly. But my body wasn't ready for that sudden change – I hadn't trained at this new pace. In retrospect, I think I tore a muscle. I quickly real-ized that I was not running my own race anymore, but trying to compete with others. So, I slowed down, focusing on finishing the race at my own pace, albeit a tad slower than I had initially hoped for. Yet as I reached the finish line, the pain and fatigue were overshadowed by the sight of my wife and children cheering for me.

Upon some post-race reflection, I learned that those who had passed me were seasoned marathoners with years of experience under their belts. I could have easily gotten sidetracked, trying to match their pace, but the race taught me an invaluable lesson: **Run your own race, at your own**

pace, and the journey will be just as rewarding as the destination.

Without commitment, you'll never start, and without consistency, you'll never finish. Remember to treat this business as a business. "I'm not a businessman, I'm a business, man!" - Jay Z.

Embarking on a career in real estate isn't merely about joining a profession; it's a journey. And much like any memorable journey, it is full of challenges, packed with learning, and marked by growth. As I look back, a few truths emerge, which I'd like to share.

1. Know Your "Why": Every action, every decision, and every sacrifice becomes purposeful when you know why you're doing it. For me, it was the dream of a better future for my family. Your "why" might be different. Cling to it. It will be your guiding star on the darkest nights.

2. Commit to Lead Generation: Dedicate at least three hours daily without fail to lead generation. I can't emphasize this enough. This single act alone can propel 75% of your success. The consistent effort, over time, will bear fruit. It's a simple formula: put in the work, and success will follow. If you're unwavering in this commitment, it's impossible not to succeed.

3. Celebrate Tiny Wins: Success isn't just about the final goal. It's about the little achievements along the way. Every client you satisfy, every house you sell, every relationship you nurture is a step towards your larger goal.

4. Your Journey is Unique: In our digital age, comparison is the thief of joy. Your journey, your pace, your story – it's all unique, and therein lies the beauty. Stay true to your path and let others inspire, not deter you.

5. Forge Ahead with Unwavering Focus: You will face challenges, market fluctuations, and tough days. With clear objectives and unyielding determination, not only will you surmount them, but you will also excel. Embracing uncertainty and adapting without always having a concrete plan is essential. Perfection in the layout of things is rare, so it's crucial to seize opportunities and take action proactively.

6. Seek a Mentor: The world of Real Estate is vast. A mentor – someone who has traversed these paths – can offer not just guidance, but also perspective, and sometimes, much-needed encouragement.

7. Invest in Continuous Learning: As the saying goes, the only constant is change. If you're not growing, you're dying. Especially in Real Estate. Keep updating your knowledge, sharpening your skills, and staying ahead of the curve.

8. Protect Your Mindset: In the face of challenges, your mindset will be your most potent weapon. Surround yourself with positivity, engage in self-care, and always be resilient. It's about learning to dance in the storm, not just weathering it.

Each Realtor® has a unique story, painted with personal challenges, marked by individual triumphs. My narrative, punctuated with highs and lows, is a testament to resilience, passion, and unyielding spirit. And as you craft your story in this industry, remember it's not about houses; it's about homes, dreams, and the lives you touch. Your legacy awaits. Embrace it one lead, one client, one home at a time.

As I look back on my career, it wasn't just about hard work. **Success in the real estate business – and life in general – is about aligning with the right people. It's about soaking in knowledge from every source, and about being prepared when opportunity knocks.** As I navigated the varied terrains of the real estate world, I quickly understood the value of mentorship, continuous learning, and keeping one's mindset unwaveringly positive.

Success is not an event or a destination. It's a journey. It's about showing up every single day, rain or shine, and giving it your all. It's about learning from each failure, celebrating each success, and believing in the journey even when the destination seems elusive. Success doesn't happen overnight. It takes time, effort, and an unyielding will to win.

The bamboo tree, in its years of growth beneath the surface before shooting up, mirrors the journey of any entrepreneur or professional. Just like the tree, our efforts may not bear visible results immediately. But with persistence, the growth is not just certain, it's exponential.

Today, as I stand at the helm of Keller Williams Realty Centres, looking back at the winding road that led me here, I'm reminded of the anonymous quote that has guided me through the most challenging times: "Do it sad, do it angry, do it miserable, do it excited, do it heartbroken, do it happy, do it tired, do it energized, do it confident, do it discouraged, do it anyway, just do it."

So, to every aspiring Realtor®, entrepreneur, or dreamer out there: your success story is waiting to be written. Forge ahead and trust the process. After all, **winning is a habit.**

KEY takeaway: **Success is equal parts hard work, effort, focus, and maximizing the opportunities and relationships you are presented with. Absorb whatever you can from all your unique interactions, and never give up on something you want to achieve.**

Find more on Colin Campbell:

www.campbellteam.ca

www.instagram.com/sircolin_campbell

www.linkedin.com/in/ColinCampbell-kwrc/

"

**YOUR BIGGEST
COMPETITION IS
THE PERSON YOU
WERE YESTERDAY.
STRIVE TO IMPROVE
EACH DAY.**

ZIG ZIGLAR

JENNA
DAVIS

🌐 jennaandkeenan.com
📷 @jennadavis_realtor
📷 @jend_48
📘 Jenna Davis Bosley Real Estate

Jenna is a proud mother of two children, ages 9 and 3. She has been with her husband Keenan for six years and he is the love of her life. She currently resides in Collingwood, Ontario, and enjoys cottaging, the beach, live music, and staying active. Jenna loves animals and has a 13-year-old miniature Australian shepherd named Echo.

Jenna has been a Realtor® for over 12 years, before which she worked in the veterinary science world. She is passionate about real estate investing and specializes in the field as well as first-time buyers and retirees. Jenna loves meeting new people and would encourage you to reach out.

CHAPTER 5
JENNA DAVIS

WHEN I WAS A LITTLE GIRL, I never dreamed about being a Realtor®, cr one day owning multiple investment properties with the desire to own an empire of them. When I was younger, I always thought that I was going to work in the animal or environmental world...which I did, for a short time. I finished high school, and like most, I didn't know what I wanted to do, so I took a year off and worked. I decided that I wanted to either be a veterinary technician or go to school for environmental studies. I got into both programs and decided to go to a veterinary tech school, specializing in wildlife.

I moved up to New Liskeard, Ontario, and started school. I took a three-year program and started working at a veterinary clinic right out of college. I bought my first property while I was in college, and that opened my eyes to what real estate is, and the power of it. It wasn't anything spectacular, but I bought a little bungalow for $110,000, lived in it for two years, and sold it for $120,000. I thought it was the greatest thing that we had done nothing and made $10,000 from it.

My partner and I took that money and decided to move to Collingwood, Ontario to buy our next place and use that $10,000 to help with a down payment.

I worked as a Veterinary Technician for about a year in Collingwood, when I soon realized that this was not what I wanted to do. The job was too slow-paced, and I hated staying in one place all day long. I found it extremely boring and unstimulating.

After purchasing my first place, real estate was always in the back of my mind and I had some curiosity about the field. I began watching shows on Home and Garden Television (HGTV) regularly, which piqued my interest even more.

After a weekend at the cottage with my family, I mentioned to my mom that 'vet tech' life wasn't for me and I needed to do something different. I was extremely lucky to have supportive parents after just getting out of college a year before that. She encouraged me to spread my wings. She and I always talked about real estate, and I had mentioned to her that I had been thinking about looking into it. My mom was all for it and told me to call on Monday and enrol in the courses! So I thought...*what the heck!* And I went for it.

I quit my vet tech job, and I continued to bartend full-time while I got my license. It took me about one year to complete all the necessary courses. While doing that I went to about five different brokerages, interviewing them in search of the right brokerage for me.

I landed at Royal LePage Trinity Realty, based out of Collingwood, right around the corner from my house. It was perfect. My Broker of Record, Dale Tkatch, was my mentor and he was very special to me. He brought real estate sales to life for me and taught me a lot.

Now, there are a few things that I would have done differently, now that I have the gift of hindsight. I had absolutely no idea about selling real estate or about business in general. I had a background in science and this was all so new to me. Knowing what I now know, I would have hired a like-minded coach who I got along well with, and who had a similar lifestyle and mindset as I did. I believe this would have jump-started my career a lot faster. I took tons of courses, I asked a lot of questions, and I had a mentor in the office that I met with once a week. She would give me tasks and "homework" to work on and we would critique it the following week. I hosted a lot of open houses, knocked on doors, and made "For Sale By Owner" packages. You name it, I did it, and I loved every minute of it!

I remember the first open house I hosted with a colleague on a long weekend in May. I wasn't thrilled about it because I usually go to the cottage that weekend, but I knew I had to push myself and start learning the business even if it was on weekends when I didn't want to work. My colleague and I sat in the open house. She did some work on her computer, and I didn't have any work to do, so I just read a book.

She said: "I'll take the first person who walks in and show you how to interact with them, and then the next one after that is all yours!" I was so nervous. I remember when that second person came in I went to go say hello and shook their hand. The buyer commented on how clammy my hands were and told me to take a deep breath. He could see from a mile away how nervous I was and that I was new to the business. I was pretty embarrassed.

I was doing everything I could to get that first client. I was sending out letters to everyone I knew, I was making follow-up calls – even to my own father-in-law! – and I still think to this day that he must've thought I was a little crazy on that call!

Although it was challenging most days working during the day as a Realtor® and at the restaurant at night, it was the restaurant that gave me my very first listing! I was so

excited. A colleague was renting out a place close by, knew the landlords wanted to sell, and he recommended me and they called me.

Okay…now what?! I had this listing appointment with the owners of a chalet in the Blue Mountain area, and I had no idea what to do. Although I loved my brokerage, they didn't have a ton of training for new agents, so I was kind of just thrown to the wolves and had to figure it out. So, I got the address, drove by to get a good idea of what it was, and asked some questions over the phone. I had also been over to my colleague's place before, so I had seen the basement apartment he was living in. I went home, printed off a ridiculous amount of comparables, and went off to my listing appointment.

I ended up getting the listing! It was such a proud moment for me. The "For Sale" sign was up, and seeing my name for the first time as an official Realtor® was a special moment. I was doing *all the things*, and it was great!

(Looking back, if I had had a coach at that time, I would have been far more prepared for the appointment, with a full listing package, and I would have had far more knowledge about the process, which in turn, would have given me more confidence going into it. But, you live and you learn!) To make a long story short, I didn't end up selling that house in the end. This was back in 2010, and the market was extremely slow. It expired, and they took it off the market and re-listed it a year or two later with another agent. (I realize now…not keeping in touch with them was another rookie mistake!)

I didn't sell my first property until I was in the business for about eight months, and then from there, I had to wait for the closing, which can be a long process. It was a buyer who bought in Wasaga Beach, Ontario, and to this day, it was the most challenging client I have ever had. Back then, being so new and not having the confidence that I needed was very hard. I didn't know how to advocate for myself and respectful agent-to-client interactions. So in the end, this was a very difficult client to deal with, but I learned a lot from that deal. The client made me work and research every little thing for that property. That experience began to give me the confidence I needed to start becoming the Realtor® I am today.

Every deal will teach you something, especially the difficult ones! This is what I love so much about real estate. There is always something new to learn, you're never in one place for long, you have the flexibility of creating your own schedule, and you dictate how much money you make depending on how hard you want to work.

At this early stage in my real estate career, I lived a pretty simple life. I didn't have many bills or debt, and I was content with making $60,000 annually. I had a partner who made a similar annual salary and combined we were stress-free and didn't have a desire to make much more. I worked independently for my first 4-5 years in real estate. I had my first child around my 5th year in real estate, and I decided that I wanted to take most of the year off and stay home with my baby. So I did!

This was such a special time for me, as life was much simpler back then. I was able to be present with my daughter, be home, and not stress about money. I think I may have sold about five houses during the year that I was home with her. Once my daughter was into part-time daycare, which didn't happen until she was about 18 months old, I started to get back into the real estate world more.

Being away from it for that long definitely took a toll on my business and it was almost like starting over again, but with a baby! A lot has changed since then. Our Broker of Record had suddenly died, which turned the whole office upside down. The company was sold to a brokerage from out of town, and it slowly started to lose its appeal. It no longer felt like "family" and the brokerage was falling behind on the newest tech.

I decided to leave the company not only for a more modern brokerage but to join a team so that I could get the help behind the scenes that I needed. I was finding it hard to juggle mom life and Realtor® life. I started with another Royal LePage brokerage in town with a team of about eight people. I worked under a married couple who specialized in luxury properties in the Blue Mountain area and felt this could be a really good fit. They had a team that did all the photos, and paperwork, helped with emails, and sign installations. These were all of the things I was having trouble keeping up with.

I worked with this team for about three years. It served its purpose at the time, but as I started to grow more and more as a Realtor®, I realized that I may not want to work under anyone and was missing being my own boss and not answering to anyone. Marketing my *own* brand was something I wanted to do as well. I was working so hard, and marketing for someone else no longer made sense to me.

A new opportunity came to me, as well as four others on the team, to join Bosley Real Estate, opening up a new office here in Southern Georgian Bay. At the time, my second child was about six months old, and I was not planning on making any major changes until he was a bit older...but as life seems to work, this was when the opportunity came my way. It was scary not only moving from the Royal LePage brand that I had grown to know and love my whole career but also starting and opening a whole new brokerage in the area with a six-month-old baby. I was a little concerned, but deep down it felt right with the people I was with and I couldn't turn down the opportunity.

That was two years ago this past July 2023. We now have 10 Realtors® as a part of our Bosley team. We have a very unique relationship as we all work independently but are very close to one another as a team and function as such. It really is the best of both worlds! We now have two offices:

one in Thornbury, Ontario, and the other – which is our new sales centre – is in Collingwood, Ontario. We have grown immensely and now have a team manager, and extreme presence in the Southern Georgian Bay. Joining this team was by far the best decision of my career!

In my experience, accepting risks and opportunities that come my way is how I've been able to grow, develop, and succeed personally and professionally. Pushing myself out of my comfort zone is something that I continuously want to do and real estate has given me the confidence to do that in all aspects of my life. It has made me who I am today, which is a knowledgeable, confident, and grateful human being!

Over the last few years, I've also begun my real estate investing career. I always knew the power of real estate, but I never knew about the magic of investing until I joined the Keyspire real estate investing community. I was able to keep the first property I bought in Collingwood, making it into two units and renting out both. My husband and I purchased our second investment property last year, and we just finished renovating it, adding a second unit. We love the Southern Georgian Bay area and are looking to purchase many more properties to come. We love the idea of creating more housing for the community, as well as creating a third business between the two of us.

Sumarlie Investments is our real estate investing company, and we are working every day to grow the business so that one day we can solely invest in real estate and step back from our other business'. Real estate investing has given us the goal of early retirement and enjoying life right now. We do not want to wait until we are 65 to retire and travel. We want to do it now while we are young, with our kids, so that we soak up every moment we can as a family.

I've learned that life is too short. Our society has prioritized an unreasonably fast-paced lifestyle, where all we're expected to do is live to work our 9-5 jobs, 8 hours per day, with one or two weeks off every a year. That lifestyle is not what we want for our family. We want time, freedom, schedule flexibility, and real estate has afforded us the ability to have just that. We love helping other people establish this kind of lifestyle, too, and we are always looking for like-minded people who want to join the real estate investing world, partner with us, and grow alongside our portfolio!

Working in this industry can involve difficult days, stagnant periods, difficult conversations, months without consistent pay cheques, and crazy expenses most don't know about or understand...but I would not change it for any other career. Real estate has given me the confidence to be who I am, to say what I need to say and to work the hardest I ever have.

If you are just getting started in the real estate landscape, or if you are thinking about joining the real estate community, I will tell you this: being a Realtor® is extremely difficult, yet rewarding. You must have a hard shell and know who you are as a person. The lifestyle it can give you is extraordinary, as long as you can create a good work-life balance, making sure to not drown yourself in the work.

Work hard when you're working, but don't forget to take time for your loved ones, your friends, and yourself.

KEY takeaway: The life you planned out for yourself isn't always the one you're meant to live. Pay attention to what lights you up, and make changes based on your strengths and passions.

Find more on Jenna Davis:

www.jennaandkeenan.com

www.instagram.com/jennadavis_realtor

www.instagram.com/jend_48

www.facebook.com/JennaDavisBosleyRealEstate

"

SUCCESS ISN'T GIVEN, IT'S EARNED. STAY FOCUSED, STAY HUNGRY, AND YOUR EFFORTS WILL PAY OFF.

GRANT CARDONE

JENNIFER JONES

Jennifer Jones leads "The Jennifer Jones Team" which has been climbing to the top of The Toronto Real Estate Board and the Top of eXp Realty Teams. Jennifer's strength lies in her skill of attracting talented leaders who help build the strategies and systems required to create a model that can be duplicated to help any agent create individual success or structure their own team to be successful.

Jennifer and her husband, Keith, own multiple rental properties and invest in storage units and commercial property throughout North America. Jennifer is a Public Speaker, Coach, and Best-Selling Author. She and her husband currently reside in King City, Ontario with their standard poodle, Mike. They enjoy time with their two grown children and recent grandchildren.

CHAPTER 6
JENNIFER JONES

I DIDN'T GROW up dreaming that I would become a real estate agent. When a psychic once told me that I would become a Realtor® and have many other businesses developing from that role, I laughed out loud and said, "No way." I never envisioned myself becoming one of "those" people. I imagined the "commission breath" sales-people with the cheap suits that I ran away from every time.

By 2005, I had invested in real estate with my previous partner for years. We purchased condos, renovated and flipped them, and would hold a few homes and condos as rental properties and investments. At the same time, I was in the gaming industry, purchasing horses both privately and from auctions, retraining and marketing them, and selling them all over North America. When the Ontario Lottery Gaming Corporation (OLG) changed the purse structures in Ontario and the future of horse racing looked grim, I walked away from it. I had been involved for seven years and had so many people I loved and respected in that business. It was a difficult decision to make, and I wasn't sure what I was going to do career-wise once I decided to depart.

After my first husband and I parted ways shortly afterward, on a personal level, I had been searching for who I liked to call, "Mr. Magic." This is someone I imagined would partner with me on all levels – spiritually, mentally, and physically. (I called this idea the "tripod" relationship because it would require all three legs to remain standing.) I had seen him in a dream years earlier shortly after my best friend had passed along with her boyfriend in a tragic Delta Comair Crash in Lexington, Kentucky. She had come to me in the dream and shown me who I would marry. It was so vivid, so real. It was not like a regular dream where you wake up and it fades. The memory is just as strong today as it was when it first happened. Maybe you have experienced something like this too?

"Mr. Magic" is the tangible manifestation of my now-partner, Keith. When I saw him, I knew he was the ONE. Now, it did take me some time to get him on board with this idea, but eventually, he could see what I saw and we partnered together in life. He was a full-time fire captain and worked a second job as a full-time contractor for a well-established builder in our area and had been doing so successfully for over twenty-five years.

Keith had separated from his wife a year prior and was a full-time father to his five-year-old son. He lived in a town-home at the time, and we sold his property to move out to a power-of-sale cottage. We purchased the cottage in a special place called Stoney Lake. We worked on the cottage, living there for an entire year with the children as we worked on creating a life together.

While going through the process of selling the cottage, we discovered we were doing a lot of the work in preparing and selling the property ourselves. We needed to sell it as we wanted to move back to York Region, and we were coming up with lots of creative ways to get the cottage sold. At this point, I realized that it just made sense for me to be licensed as a Realtor® as we discovered this would be a way for us to build wealth together and hold on to more of the "sweat equity" that went into the projects.

We moved back to York Region into a home on Lake Simcoe and fostered children while I was unintentionally building a real estate business. In the beginning, it was not a purposeful act. As we sold our properties, we had others around us ask us to represent them, and it was then that I realized I loved the challenge of it. I dove in head first.

I was a new Realtor® in a small town where a few local agents had dominated for decades. I focused on just adding value to others, being of service, and visualizing my success. Keith and I drove to the lakefront every morning, sipping on our Tim Hortons coffee, and in my mind, I would declare: "I am so grateful for all the buyers and sellers that come my way." After doing this for a year, almost all the signs along the lakefront were mine. I declared at the end of my second year in real estate that I would make 1 million dollars the next year. That's easier to do today, but seven years ago with an average price point of $550,000, it was not quite so easy. I hired my first assistant, leased a small office in town, and took over the area. I spent all of my time anticipating what my clients needed. I worked to put into place systems that would address their needs before they knew they had them. I focused on being generous and providing the same high level of service, regardless of whether it was a lease or a million-dollar lakefront home.

At the end of my third year in the business, I had made over 1 million dollars. I was now overflowing with new business and finding it challenging to provide that same high level of service since it was more work than one person could handle. Another local agent whom I aligned with came asking to join my team. She consistently kept asking until one day I agreed. That's how the team was born!

Once my team was set up, more agents joined us and at the end of that year, even though we had made a lot of money, I had lost $150,000. That's the danger of working in the business and not "on" the business. I had to go back to my team, admit that I had failed them, and change my commission splits. I sent my amazing office manager, Sarah, (my first hire who was now licensed and answering all my prayers) to Austin, Texas to shadow the top team at that time in our company. I realized there was no point re-inventing the wheel, and this team had declared bankruptcy before and was now thriving and super profitable. I was determined to help my team learn from the best, and doing so by linking arms with other successful agents was the best way forward. Sarah came home, implemented all of the same systems into our team, and we were off to the races.

The team grew from there to almost thirty Realtors®. We were the dominant team at our brokerage, and number two within Canada. Once the brokerage was running reasonably smoothly, I realized was bored. (That's the plague of the entrepreneur, isn't it!?) We love starting businesses, setting up systems and processes, and then moving to the next challenge. I decided what made sense was to open a brokerage within our franchise, so I approached our broker/owner. I was told no. Everywhere. You can't go into that area, someone owns it, etc, etc. I told our brokerage owner and a few other key people in the company, "If I don't have an opportunity here, I will leave and find it elsewhere."

And that's what I did. I had all the top brands approaching us to open a location for them. I even considered opening our own brokerage as we were operating as our own independent island within our team office and rarely used the mothership except to go in and train others for free.

I was blessed to be in the top 200 agents globally for the company and would fly down quarterly to attend Gary Keller's top agent mastermind. It was a great mastermind but there was no one-on-one time with Gary, only a one-minute photo opportunity. Within the top-agent group, we had a Facebook group as well, and gradually over a few years, I watched top teams and top individual agents leaving. Every time that happened, I would look up the agent in question and realized they were all going to one brokerage: 'eXp Realty.' I knew nothing about that firm, other than Gary referencing it in the sessions, calling it "Donkey Kong," insinuating that it was not a reputable brand.

That's when I started taking a closer look. I could see within the model that it was very "agent-centric." It focused on rewarding the top producers in the company by giving them the commission they paid to "cap" back to them once they hit certain production levels and cultural give-backs within the company. Basically, top producers had a free ride. They also gave the agents "ownership" through stock and allowed them to share in the equity as well. The agents all had multiple income streams – and many of the income streams were passive.

So I moved to eXp Realty… and my team started exploding. More and more agents approached me to join and we created our own in-house 'JJ Team Boot Camp' program. eXp excused all our joining agents from their company boot camp as we ran our own and we became experts at turning out agents who were super successful as long as they followed our program to the letter.

Success in real estate is surface-level simple…yet, it's complex as well. You first need the right personality. You need to be likeable. The second thing you need is the right mindset. Whether you believe you can succeed or not, you're right. The third trait you need is a desire to learn and grow. To be successful, become a sponge and learn as many new things as you can because this business is always changing and you need the ability to recognize it and pivot accordingly. The fourth thing you need is the desire to serve and please others. The customer is always right. Period. Learn to take responsibility for everything that goes wrong. Would you rather be right or be rich? (And I don't say rich because money is important to me… in fact, it's not. I'm more concerned with what I can do to help those around me. I love experiences. I love to travel. Material things have no real value to me, but they do to Keith. He sees cars, nice homes, and expensive things as evidence of hard work and the sacrifices we have made.

And I love to see Keith happy. I also love to be able to give back to my family and friends without limits. We all have our own individual preferences!)

This new brokerage has provided me with unlimited opportunities to grow, evolve, and scale my business to unlimited levels. Running this business has put me on stages and has given me multiple speaking platforms which in turn gives me the credibility I need to expand our business even further and help more agents succeed. My goal is always to provide *them* with opportunities to develop into leaders without "clipping their wings" like in a traditional team model.

Now, we are still connected to our international brokerage. I created a weekly training calendar with the top Canadians on it, helping share information from the top individuals and top teams with splashes of other international content. Our team has grown to over fifty amazing Realtor®, and I have an ever-expanding group of Realtors® and teams that I support and mentor in my organization. I spend a lot of time running real estate events based on collaboration, not competition. I also do a lot of speaking on international stages. Our team sits at number 7 out of 70,000 Realtors® on one of the largest boards in the world, the Toronto Regional Real Estate Board (TRREB).

Through creating systems and processes for everything and pouring into others without the focus on what I receive in return, my whole world has changed. I see the future, and the future is bright.

KEY takeaway: You don't have to do things the same way as everybody else does. If the same systems we have used in the past to grow, aren't always the ones that lead

to new opportunities. Keep an open mind and investigate new paths – you never know where they can lead!

Find more on Jennifer Jones:

www.jj.team

www.instagram.com/jenniferjonesrealestateteam

THE ONLY PLACE WHERE SUCCESS COMES BEFORE WORK IS IN THE DICTIONARY.

VIDAL SASSOON

JENNIFER SILBERNAGEL

Jennifer Silbernagel has been a licensed real estate agent since February 2006, having worked in various roles within the industry, including administrative assistant, buyer agent, seller agent, income property specialist, team member, manager, leasing agent, property manager, productivity coach, and team owner. Jennifer is committed to motivating her clients to achieve new heights and fostering a learning-based, supportive environment for agents. With extensive experience, Jennifer offers diverse perspectives on real estate business and agent roles.

For the past decade, Jennifer has been actively teaching and coaching in real estate, deeply passionate about assisting agents in efficiently managing and growing their businesses while boosting productivity and income.

CHAPTER 7
JENNIFER SILBERNAGEL

WHEN I WAS GROWING UP, my parents owned multiple-income properties and homes they had flipped over the years. I spent many summers helping to paint, clean up, or shop for those homes with my mom. I was raised around certain elements of the real estate industry and investment properties, and I think that is where my passion for property sales stems from.

I was a strong student and made my way to Toronto from Niagara to complete my Bachelor's Degree. It didn't take me long to realize that I was not built to be a full-time student. I wanted freedom, flexibility, money, and to call my own shots. I told my parents I wanted to drop out of school. I was done writing essays. I was done with class-rooms and exams. I wanted to get out there and work. The only work I knew I loved was working on and renovating properties. (In hindsight, I can see that the idea of me dropping out of school was a shock for my parents. I was a strong student, and they felt I needed a degree to get ahead in life. I had worked so hard already. They weren't wrong; they were worried. So, we agreed to a compromise. I would move home to Niagara, finish my degree in three years, and get my real estate license at the same time. I had my plan, and I executed it.)

By this time, I was 21 years old with little life experience and even less knowledge of what it meant to be a successful Real Estate Agent. During my last year at school, I worked as an assistant for my mom's Realtor®, so I was exposed to the business a little and knew what the paperwork and processes were like. I believe this opportunity was one of the reasons I was able to be so successful right out of school. I sold 12 homes in my first year as an agent and was Rookie of the Year at my respective brokerage. I was hustling to do open houses and take phone duty any chance I could get. I was building a very successful business that I loved!

That next fall, with a little help from my parents, I bought my first home. It was an older cottage down by the water and it needed some love. So I took the savings I had from my home sales and we worked to renovate that property into *my* first home. It was small and sweet and I was so proud to call it my own. I felt that I was missing something, though, and I didn't know for a while what that was.

While I worked I kept trying to figure out what I needed and one day it all just kind of…clicked. I don't know why or how I realized this, I just kind of knew it was right. I loved my job, my house, my colleagues, my family…and I didn't want to upset anyone, but I was not living in the right place. I was bored. I wanted a busier lifestyle and I wanted more opportunities. This realization led me to one of the biggest changes in my life. I found myself an apartment, packed the stuff I was able to bring with me, and moved myself back to Toronto. I didn't know how this would turn out. I had no guarantee and about $7000 in my bank account...but I was sure it was the right thing for me, so I made it happen.

During this time, I also found tenants for my home and started renting it out while I got myself settled in Toronto as a licensed assistant. After about a year, once I learned more about the Greater Toronto Area markets and how to approach their real estate negotiations, I was offered the opportunity to jump back into sales. At the time, I said no because I was comfortable and it was easy for me to stay where I was with some opportunity for growth on the administrative side of the industry.

This is one of the biggest lessons I carry with me from this time. If my business partner had not sat me down and told me what the opportunity truly was, and if I had let the fear of "100% commission" hold me back, I would not have grown to be a top-producing agent across Keller Williams Canada. I would not have grown to be a top producer in my office, to be a leader in my office, and eventually to start my own coaching company.

My time in this role, working beside a broker-owner and eventually growing to partner with him and run our real estate business, was a ten-year journey. I was a sponge during those years. I went to every training and all of the conventions and courses I could. I spent that time investing in my skills and mind while I worked hard in the business.

I started as a younger agent, and while many saw this as a setback, I saw it as a challenge to conquer. When I look back now on those years, I can see how that hustle paid off. The evenings, weekends, late nights, and early mornings, were my education in real estate. Many were hard; some were exciting; all were instrumental in creating the opportunities that would start coming my way.

What I started to learn about myself as I grew into a leader in our brokerage was that agents were naturally drawn to me for support, assistance, training, and general consultation. I enjoyed those moments more than the wins at the offer table, or the daily hustle of real estate. I was searching for more and I felt a little lost at this time. I made the difficult decision to step away from my partnership. It wasn't easy, and again, I was afraid of leaving the comfort and the support I had in that partnership. It was also the right decision. I needed to start to carve my own trail.

I started coaching as a Productivity Coach within the brokerage, working with new agents to help them build their businesses and get started in their careers. I started building a real estate team, but I found that I loved the coaching element even more; it was a natural place for me to be and I felt that I was naturally good at it. Those agents' wins felt like they were my wins – sometimes even better than mine – and I knew that meant something big for me. I just didn't know what the path was…yet. I felt that I was supposed to build a team because I was an agent, after all, and that is what successful agents traditionally do. So I partnered with another agent and we set out to build a vision for a team. It worked, for a while. We built a successful, top-producing team quite quickly, however, I found that when I slowed down and looked around, I was doing a lot of the deals, the coaching, the building... and things were a bit out of alignment for me.

During this time, my personal life was also starting to take up a larger space in my world. I was engaged and looking to move out of the city to a more suburban area, and I was very excited about it. I had been working hard and hustling for a long time and I was tired. We had also moved homes and we moved brokerages with the team. I believe I hit a point where I needed a break and a change of pace. I realized that the partnership I was in with my team was not the right one for me. It was a hard realization to make. I had to choose to walk away from three years of building, of growth, of capital investment, and success. I made that decision because I knew that it was best for me and my future opportunities, but that one really stung. The funny thing is, though, when you realize what the problem is, all of a sudden solutions start to show up – and that is exactly what happened to me.

Around the same time that I was looking to step away from my team and start over...again...the manager of our office came to me with an opportunity to build a new Productivity Coaching program from scratch within our brokerage. It was perfect for me. It was a break from the day-to-day, it was my real passion, and it was a reason to step away from the team. How could I say no? (I couldn't!)

Over the next three years, I worked hard to build a program that trained agents to be top producers in our brokerage and to run successful businesses. It worked, and it is the best program or business I have built to date. This is the thing I am most grateful for. My coaching program is still running in our brokerage. We work with over 60 agents. We coach top-producing teams, brand-new agents, and everybody in between. We help agents change their lives and run businesses they love with more structure and better vision than I ever had. We create amazing relationships within our company and I have had the opportunity to bring on two of our own coaching agents as coaches whom I get to work with on a daily basis. It's such a joy to see them grow and learn new skills as well.

My husband partnered with me on this adventure when we decided to have children (we have two now, Brooke and Owen) and we have been able to continue growing our brand while staying in an industry we love. We have purchased three homes, renovated and sold two of them, and managed to make our way into our favourite neighbourhood and obtain a home we love because we wanted to keep using real estate as a vehicle for wealth. We were able to buy our first cottage last year (a goal of ours for many years), and now we get to enjoy it as a family and also benefit from it functioning as an occasional Airbnb rental. All of this was happening while my husband continued to run a very successful real estate team with his parents because we were certain that we needed to keep moving forward. We needed to keep momentum and we didn't want to stop and rest in the middle of our growth.

Over the past year-and-a-half, my journey has led me to a new, uncomfortable (yet exciting!) opportunity. I accepted the role of Team Leader at our brokerage. My coaches are now running the program and excelling, and I felt that I needed to push myself. When the opportunity was presented to me, I was forced to look back and think over why I would make another change and look forward to where I wanted to go next. What I learned from this retrospection was that in every moment when I was comfortable, when I wanted to keep things status quo or was afraid of the change, I took the challenge anyway. Each of those decisions has led me to a bigger win or a bigger opportunity. I didn't know what the outcome of accepting this new challenge would be – I still don't – but I do know that it is the right path for me because it is uncertain, it is new, and I have the opportunity to learn more and do something big. The fun part for me is figuring out the win, and as long as I keep looking for new ways to win, I will be just fine.

My advice: If you are comfortable, you are not challenging yourself and you need to push yourself into a space that challenges you. All of our growth comes from those uncertain spaces. If you can learn to live and work in those lanes, you will grow faster and bigger than the people around you who choose comfort.

KEY takeaway: Get comfortable with being uncomfortable. That's where growth lives, and challenging your comfort zone is how you expand.

Find more on Jennifer Silbernagel:

www.instagram.com/jennsilbernagel

LIANNE TIMBERS-SHARP

🌐 **liannesharp.ca**
📘 **Lianne Timbers Sharp**
📷 **@timberssharp_sells**

Lianne is no stranger to challenges. She embraces change and has worked to build a successful career as a Realtor® over the past seven years. Lianne was educated at McMaster University, and holds a Bachelor of Science in Psychology, along with a Bachelor of Science in Occupational Therapy. She has been a licensed Occupational Therapist for almost 30 years and continues to run a private practice while working full-time as a Realtor®.

Although originally from Milton, Ontario, Lianne spent most of her adult life in Grimsby before finally relocating her life and businesses to the Bruce Peninsula area in 2023. Lianne has competed in many triathlons, including two Ironman races. She loves to spend time outdoors with her dog, Maisey and enjoys volunteering in the community, hiking on the Bruce Trail, meditating down by the water, and working with others in their health and wellness path.

CHAPTER 8
LIANNE TIMBERS-SHARP

CHANGE. We need it to grow. We need it to develop. We crave it. We fear it. Some are stuck and terrified, while others take the steps and embrace the risks. Who am I? Am I a risk taker, or do I prefer to play it safe? In my past, I've played it safe. I've done what I was "supposed" to do. I went to university, graduated with an Honours Degree in Psychology, and then went on to get a professional degree in Occupational Therapy. I worked in healthcare as a successful Occupational Therapist. I got married. My husband and I bought a house. We had a family. We sold our first house, bought a bigger house, and moved to Grimsby to live closer to family, and to raise our children in a small town. Life was good...or so I thought.

As time went on, I realized I was struggling with the comfortable lifestyle I had created. My marriage was beyond repair, so I pushed myself outside of my comfort zone and started the process of change. I got divorced. I bought my own home. I continued to work in healthcare. I pushed myself as an athlete. Life was good...*or so I thought.*

As a seasoned Occupational Therapist, I was regularly out in the community and visiting my clients inside their homes. As much as the career was rewarding, it came with its own challenges – many times these challenges were due to certain provincial regulations and changing government systems over the years in Ontario. I loved the work I was doing, but I felt that something was missing. There were certain elements to the job that I loved – I was constantly on the move, which kept me interested and focused, and some parts of the job allowed for at-home, remote work. If I were to make a massive change and shift careers, I knew that I needed something that would give me this same type of flexibility, variety, and movement. I wasn't sure what that was, though.

The lightbulb went on for me during the spring of 2015. I was training for my first Ironman Triathlon at the time. I was also newly engaged and planning our wedding for August of the same year. I was busting my ass to get in the 25-30 homecare visits per week that I needed to earn a reasonable income, when one day, I met a man who changed my life trajectory. He wasn't the man of my dreams (I was already engaged to him!), but he became the person who prompted me to take one of the biggest risks of my life.

I met him when I was seeing his mother as a home care client. Every time I went to their home, he was there, dressed in a dress shirt and track pants. He drove a BMW and lived in a beautiful home on Lake Ontario. When I finally asked him what he did for work, he told me he was a Real Estate Agent. THAT WAS THE MOMENT I KNEW WHAT I WAS GOING TO DO! I will never forget that moment. I could see it clearly in front of me! We talked about the process of getting licensed and I was hooked!

I had always loved decorating, design, and of course, had seen more houses during my home care career than any real estate agent would ever see! I had worked with every kind of person and personality. I had experienced situations and living conditions that most people never experience. I had spent my career negotiating with people to make changes in their lives to facilitate their independence and safety. I had worked with the most stubborn and the most flexible. As a regulated healthcare professional, I understood and practiced the critical elements of transparency, honesty, and integrity.

I knew I needed a change and I knew I wanted to work for myself and reap the benefits of my hard work. I wanted to meet people and be in different environments all the time. I wanted to be able to do work from home. I wanted to be able to take time off without having to request it. I wanted to use all the skills, experience, and knowledge I had accumulated after working with thousands of people in their homes to solve their problems.

Once I had made this realization, I called my fiancé right away and told him what I was going to do! He paused, and hesitantly said…*What about your OT career? What about your education and all the time and energy you've put into your career? What about your income?* I stopped the car and took a breath. Was I going to let the fear of change control me? His concerns were valid…what if real estate didn't work out? How would I do all the courses while working full-time? Would I quit my full-time job and give up that income to take a chance selling houses? How would I sell houses? How would I meet people? Would people trust me? WHAT IF I COULDN'T MAKE ANY MONEY? I was 45 years old... was it too late to start something new?

The questions flooded my head...but I knew I could do this! I started the process of change years ago when I decided to get divorced. I had pushed myself when I decided to compete in triathlons. I had set a crazy goal of doing an Ironman. So, I took my Occupational Therapist brain and went through the process of breaking down the steps of becoming a real estate agent. (We call this "task analysis" in the OT world.) I sat in my car and calmly thought it all through.

1. Get married in August.

2. Complete the Muskoka Ironman.

3. Look into the real estate courses.

4. Talk with real estate agents about the good, the bad, and the ugly.

5. Take the courses over the next year.

6. In September 2016, start at a brokerage and continue to do home care.

Was I crazy? Could I seriously continue my home care career AND build a business in real estate? This was going to be nuts. I sat my family down and told them we had to work together so that I could make this dream come true. Everyone was on board and excited. I was excited.

And so, it began!

The wedding was amazing. The Ironman was unbelievable. The real estate courses were interesting, and the challenges of "adult" learning became evident! I quickly learned that the skills I developed in university came in very handy. Study notes, cue cards, and late nights as a "student" were the norm. I worked full-time during the day and studied at night. My teenagers and new husband embraced their roles around the house so I could focus on my dream.

I hadn't taken an exam since 1995. I remember driving to Mohawk College, terrified that I would fail. Multiple-choice, often referred to as multiple-guess, had always been daunting to me. I sat down in a room filled with people of all ages, took a deep breath, wiped off my sweaty hands, and dove into the questions. I never looked back. Each course and exam provided a little more knowledge and a little more insight into the world of real estate. I aced all the exams and met some great friends during the in-class sessions. I didn't let fear hold me back!

By September 2016, I had completed all of the required education and tests and had decided on the brokerage I was going to become a part of. At 46 years old with one career under my belt, I was starting something new, with people I didn't know, in a field I knew nothing about. (I managed to ace the courses, but real life is totally different!)

I chose my brokerage because it was a small office and the agent I had used personally through buying and selling had agreed to be my mentor. I knew I needed to be in an office where I could ask questions and feel comfortable admitting that I didn't know something. Everyone was amazing and I never felt alone during the two years I was there.

At the time, the safety of a small brokerage was what I needed, but after gaining some experience and recognizing the importance of efficient, progressive systems, I knew it was time for another change. I was ready to take another leap into a larger brokerage. As daunting as that felt at the time, I went for it, and again didn't let fear hold me back.

I made that change and my business continued to grow significantly. From 2016 to 2018, I continued to work in home care full-time while simultaneously selling real estate full-time. At the end of 2018, I knew it was time to give up my home care position. I had just changed brokerages and now had systems in place that would help me grow. I felt confident that I could make it work, even though there was always that tiny voice in the back of my head questioning my decision to quit home care. I asked myself, "What's the worst thing that could happen?" and the answer wasn't as scary as I anticipated. I was not giving up my OT license, so I would always have something to fall back on.

I leaped, and my business grew substantially. Life was good... *or so I thought.*

Fast-forward to August of 2019. I was preparing to do a second Ironman in Mount Tremblant. My husband and I went with our friend to her dad's cottage on the Bruce Peninsula for a weekend away. There happened to be a few vacant lots for sale on the water. We had just lost a good friend in a drowning accident and were really reviewing life and what was truly important. After looking at one of the lots, I spent the 3.5-hour drive home to Grimsby talking to my husband about how we could purchase our own lot. I didn't stop talking. By the time we were home, I had it all figured out.

My dream has always been to own property and essentially get away from the golden horseshoe/GTA area. This was our opportunity to get land – and it was on the water. Even better!

By October 2019, we were the proud owners of two acres on the water, on the Bruce Peninsula. I thought we would just camp there now and again, but we quickly found out that wasn't an option. My husband couldn't wait for us to build. Again, we had no idea how that process worked or where the money would come from.

We built our cottage during the COVID-19 pandemic in 2020. Our builder was incredible. On March 5, 2021, we received the keys and walked into our new cottage. I fell in love immediately! I knew at that very moment that I wanted to spend every minute there that I could.

Over the next year, we lived a very stressful life dealing with our new condo townhouse build in Smithville and driving back and forth to the cottage. My husband was very fortunate as he could flex his hours and go to the cottage from Thursday to Monday each week. I, however, did not have this flexibility. Real estate can be all-consuming. There are no set hours and if you aren't available, you don't make money. I would drive four hours to the cottage hoping to get a day or two there, and then had to turn around the next day to show houses. My clients were very understanding, and my colleagues helped where they could. The more I did this, the more I resented my career in real estate, and my husband, who could go enjoy and relax.

In 2022, I decided it was time for another change. I brought up the idea to my husband about moving to our cottage full-time and selling real estate on the peninsula. He thought I was nuts. Again, understandably, he had many questions. I knew the easy answer was to stay doing what I was doing, but it was killing me. I wasn't training anymore. I wasn't happy, and I wasn't satisfied.

My husband is the most supportive person I know and he is my rock. He 100% supported me in deciding to switch my business to the Bruce Peninsula. This meant joining a new brokerage and essentially starting from scratch. I decided to join a team as I didn't have the same connections as I did at home. I knew I would need the support from people who knew the area. I also knew that I could bring value to a team with my experience and background. I haven't looked back! After a year and a half spent working on a team and having gained more clarity in my professional preferences and processes, I have taken another step outside of my comfort zone, and have set out on my own with Remax Grey-Bruce, Brokerage.

I have taken a leap many times in my life and am so thankful that I have. I wouldn't be where I am if I had let fear rule me. I wouldn't be where I am if I didn't embrace and seek out change. I don't want to be stuck. **We don't have to be stuck.**

I have found my place and continue to look for new challenges and opportunities. I am still an OT and run a very successful private practice. I use my skill set every day in every interaction and every transaction. Through understanding the needs of individuals and the importance of future planning I am able to guide decisions related to moving, modifying, and aging in place.

My motto is "Open The Door To Better Living!" and I have honour of facilitating this each and every day!

When I reflect on where I am currently in my life and career, I continue to be awestruck by what I've accomplished and how much more I can grow. I love having my hand in a few different "pots" to keep life interesting and always evolving. Real estate is a big part of that process.

Reflecting on my career as a Realtor®, I believe I have some valuable experience and knowledge to share with others.

Here are my top 10 things to remember in this career (and in all careers, really):

1. LISTEN…to your clients, your colleagues, and everyone else.

2. Always do what you say you're going to do.

3. Take pride in every relationship and transaction you are involved with.

4. When you list a property, remember, it reflects on who you are as a businessperson and individual. Put the work in. Make sure it's clean, staged, professionally photographed, and that toilet seats are down in pictures!

5. Take time with your listings to proofread your work and review each photograph.

6. Be transparent.

7. Be honest.

8. Don't be greedy.

9. Budget your money.

10. Don't let the business run your life; your marriage, children, and health are most important.

For me, real estate has never been about money. Yes, the cheques are great when they come in, but sometimes, there are big gaps and it's easy to get desperate and frustrated. Never think this is an easy career. It can take over, become all-consuming, and stressful. There are times when you must sacrifice dinners out, long weekends, and give up your own time. You must decide if you are okay with all of that and set boundaries around your personal life and business.

Be prepared to talk about real estate...A LOT! People always want to know your thoughts on the market and what their home is worth. (Sometimes I would rather talk about the weather!) And lastly, be prepared to become a marketing and social media expert while also navigating all of the administrative components.

These past eight years have been such an incredible journey that I never expected to be on. I would not change a thing and I look forward to many more years of growth in this field!

KEY takeaway: Never let fear hold you back! You never know what is on the other side of change. Take the leap and go for it.

Find more on Lianne Timbers-Sharp:

www.liannesharp.ca

www.facebook.com / LianneTimbersSharp

www.instagram.com / timberssharp_sells

MELISSA TAYLOR

🌐 melissataylorteam.ca
📷 @melissataylor_realestate
f The Melissa Taylor Team
in Melissa Taylor Real Estate
   Team

Melissa began her real estate career when her family sold their recreational resort after 38 years of service in 2011. While in the hospitality industry, Melissa served many years on the Provincial Board and sat as President for two years guiding, lobbying, and helping more than 420 families in business navigate the path to growth and overcoming challenges during one of the most intense times for this industry.

In 2020, after years as a successful single agent, Melissa created a small team of one agent and one part-time administrator. During that time, Melissa also created a second business in investing and flipping. To date, Melissa's Real Estate Team includes a full-time operations team of three salaried team members, an Inside Sales Agent company, a Virtual Assistant, and seven agents.

CHAPTER 9
MELISSA TAYLOR

NIKE HAD it right when they came out with their trademark slogan "Just Do It." Growing up wearing Nike, I would have never imagined how that slogan would become the basis of all of my successes and all of my failures in life. Those three words would have more impact than anything I could ever study or learn – about real estate and life.

The elusive "magic" that every Realtor® and business owner spends most of their time searching for is hiding in plain sight. The problem is that our eyes are always looking outward. So our search for the answers often begins with us looking externally for the skill, the talent, and the opportunities. I hope that my story will have you discovering the magic far quicker than I did and that you will realize that YOU are the key to unlocking that magic!

One month into being licensed, I received my very first commission check for a deal that I was personally involved in. A whopping $60,000.00 commission. After two agents attempted to sell my family's seasonal resort of 96 acres while I was completing the licensing process, I knew that both of them were missing the mark. I knew my hospitality business and I understood that the selling price was going to be impacted by the division of risk. I could see opportunities to bring a deal together, where the other Realtors® did not. Once licensed and when the contracts expired with those two agents, I revisited previously interested buyers, and I was able to convert one of those interested buyers to a sold owner of that 96-acre resort.

If you stop reading here, I'm sure that I sound pretty smart, successful, and resourceful. Read on and see how this was the worst thing that could have happened to me, and how I learned one of the biggest lessons in real estate. This was Spring 2011.

The ease and immediacy of this transaction firmly set in my mind that not only was I pretty good at my "job" – but it was also relatively *easy* for me. So I did what I believed every successful business person did after a successful transaction, and I rewarded myself. I set my lounge chair on the front lawn and I lay in the sun luxuriating through the entire summer. Based on my track record (of 1), I reasoned that when money gets short, I would stand up from the lawn chair, and go and sell something else.

As I was frolicking around that summer, I had no idea that as each day passed, I wasn't taking a pause, I was falling behind my potential career and success, one glorious day after the other. "Pause" doesn't exist when we speak about our goals and dreams. Your choices either move you closer to your goals or further away. Don't fool yourself into thinking that you have the power to pause.

That inevitable day when money was getting low arrived. I was up, dressed, and ready to go to help all of the families I imagined were waiting for an effective salesperson such as myself, and I finally went into the office. I was a bit shaken. Agents around me were submitting offers, were on the phones, and many were training and participating in something they called "scripting" (which sounded painful!). I felt bad that these seasoned agents were still having to "practice" while somehow I already possessed all of the skills to get the job done!

This immense falsehood that I created and believed in – of innate skill and abilities being enough to succeed – was about to pave a path to nine years of struggle, difficulty, low goals, and even lower results. Understand that by industry standards, I was thriving. I was a capper, and people who cap are celebrated! I fell into allowing the industry to determine both my level of success and what was celebrated. Where most agents wanted to bust through the cap, to where they were earning more, I would arrive at the cap mark and coast. I met that standard set for me in my mind and in doing so, I left thousands of dollars and dreams on the table. I wasn't leading my career; I was like a bowling ball in a lane with bumpers, bouncing around within the parameters that my brokerage set for me, not understanding why or how just knowing that someone somewhere had benchmarks, so my aim was for those, not for my own goals. I was an entrepreneur finding comfort in the restrictions of others. What an oxymoron!

"Seek and you shall find," Matthew 7:7 in the Bible tells us, and by gosh he was right! Look outside of yourself for the answers, and you will find many that you can add to your cache of reasons and excuses why others succeed and not yourself. The nine-year struggle began. I was learning – and conditioning myself to believe – that real estate is a grind. I would finish one deal, and only then would I go and hunt for another. It was long, it was fearful, and I was in a constant state of pain and need. I didn't see any other way except to continue the grind, only looking as far in front of me as my twitching eyes would allow me to.

I didn't yet understand many things, and compounding actions was one of those very important things. In 2019, I moved to Keller Williams as a broken agent, having started a successful flipping business while at the same time, losing my shirt as a Realtor®. Deals were collapsing like dominoes after the artificial spike and fall of the 2017 market. I crawled through those brokerage doors intent on leaving my Realtor® career behind and maintaining my license purely to use while flipping. I had failed. I was in debt, behind in my taxes, and I was hanging on by a thread emotionally.

Six little words from the woman interviewing me planted a seed in my soul that was the beginning of a drastic change. I told her that I just wanted to come to Keller Williams to die. I was finished in public real estate, and I just needed my license to do my flipping projects. Her immediate response was, "Well that's just not going to happen." This woman had no idea who I was. However…

Something I hadn't felt in a long time started to poke around the scars of my failures. Hope, curiosity, and faith are what I carried out the door that day. I had NO idea that the small glimmer that piqued my interest that day would be the foundation for all that would come after. Nike's words echoed… "Just Do It."

Don't get me wrong; I was still in a hole financially and emotionally, but it was that 2mm shift from a woman who barely knew me that had me questioning everything I had believed up to that point. I tucked my pride away like an elusive piece of chewing gum under a shoe. I became curious about all of the training that was being offered to everyone both inside and outside the brokerage, and I started saying YES.

What an eye-opener! It became clear to me fairly quickly that not only were the speakers at these seminars hugely successful, but by listening to the conversations and inter-actions around me, the caliber of the attendees was impres-sive and it was the attendees that also shared an immense amount of success. Where were the desperate and fallen, like me? They were nowhere to be found. That would become a pattern that I still observe today. *Why?* I was about to find out.

During one particular seminar in Western Ontario, a fellow Realtor®, my senior in both experience and age, recalled the success he had in his career, and followed that with the number of times he had taken the same training programs over and over. Initially, I felt sorry for him. Having to take the same program so many times to understand it seemed extreme. Then I began to hear murmurings around me of the number of times each of the agreeing agents had also repeated courses and trainings. Something clicked that day and I will be forever grateful. *The value of full immersion!*

Sharpening my craft began to change from something I HAD to do, to something I GET to do. I looked around that packed room of successful agents, and I began to feel lucky to even be there. I wanted more.

My brokerage had an opportunity for our agents to go to an international conference, where they promised to offer us amazing training and relationship building. Embarrassed to admit that I couldn't afford it, I declined. Six little words from an administrator to me in passing urged me down a path I did not expect. "You can't afford *not* to go!" Fresh off of my revelation from my last seminar, and with Nike's words firmly embedded in my mind, I took a leap of faith.

I embossed my shirt with the yet-to-be-realized "Taylor Team" and embarked on a trip I couldn't afford, to a place I was unfamiliar with...like an imposter.

It was like going through the hole Alice in Wonderland fell through. This event was HUGE. The information I learned was overwhelming! Always observant, I also noticed that the agents that were present were all extremely successful. I was starting to see a pattern.

On that trip, I was like a detective. I stayed close to those successful agents. If they were up, I was up. I was the first awake and the last to bed. Whether I was asking questions within a group, or eavesdropping on the conversations around me, I was a sponge. The relationships I made on that trip helped me realize that it is the SUCCESSFUL agents who greatly represent the attendees at these events. The actions that these Realtors® do EVERY day is what allows them to be successful. My understanding of what a successful Realtor® actually does was beginning to change.

I began my career judging my success by the number of transactions that I completed. I was slowly realizing that transactions weren't the seeds of my success, they are the harvest of well-planted seeds! **My attention had been on the result, not the process.**

I came home with my head full of new information and I began to see what was missing. I definitely had habits. Mostly bad habits that I was becoming more and more aware of. I had some good habits as well, however up to this point, I attributed those to good luck. I began to wonder if I could utilize all of the information that I learned to make those "good luck" instances repeatable. This would take discipline, as I had been telling myself some lies for quite some time. I'm a "big picture" person; the details are really interruptions. Spontaneity and authenticity were my gifts and my joy. Order, rules, and structure were my kryptonite. Boy, I can be convincing, and I believed those things about myself – for years.

Like a child who thrives with structure, I thought the same might apply. I knew that I couldn't rely on myself to get into new habits because I am very convincing, and I love to make myself right. That would be self-sabotage. I also knew that I couldn't afford to hire someone. With urging from my coach (another great lesson: every successful person I know and have met has a mentor or a coach), I agreed to hire someone with the exact opposite traits of me. Organized, detailed, and someone who loves systems. I agreed, knowing that I had a $3,000 overdraft that I could use to pay her if everything went south. That was in 2019. That beloved assistant is still with me and is now one of four salaried employees on my operations team. But I'm getting ahead of myself.

I mentioned earlier that I had embossed "Taylor Team" onto my shirt for that convention. It was tongue-in-cheek at the time, and my kids would say that I was "posing." Shortly after that convention, I kept in close contact with a Realtor® and we would talk every morning. Until one day, my husband said, *"Why don't you just start a team?"*

From my position, where I was still working hard to shovel myself out of debt, with very few deals on the books and absolutely no systems yet completed, I scoffed as I informed him what a ridiculous idea that was! I then reached out to my coach so that we could shake our heads together at this outlandish suggestion. But with my coach's three little words, my trajectory was once again going to level up. She said, "Let's build it!" which shocked and electrified my system with fear, anticipation, doubt, and excitement all at once.

I cannot stress enough how essential having a mentor or coach with you during your journey is. **You can save the money on the map, but be prepared for a much longer, bumpier road where the destination is unknown.** With fear, trepidation, and a whole lot of faith, I jumped on Nike's train, and felt from my soul that I would "Just Do It." And I knew that I wouldn't do it alone.

I had a coach, an ingenious assistant, and a supportive family, and I stepped up as any hopeful imposter would. I prayed that I would be able to lift people up and not drag them down in the firestorm that this could swiftly become. The building of that team is for another book. The lessons learned and the wins along the way would fill these pages – with both tears and laughter.

The most important thing I want to leave with you is when I began to see that I was the one who held all the magic. It all clicked for me when I discovered exactly what all of those successful agents were doing, and why it was always them who filled the seats of the many conferences and seminars that I attended. The key is understanding that the SEEDS are what you need to focus on to even have a harvest of transactions.

Success leaves clues. Repetition, practice, and proximity to who you want to become are essential. Failure leaves clues as well. Nike's "Just Do It" mantra encourages you to do things despite any limitations. FEAR is the misty curtain that hangs between what you have and EVERYTHING that you want. **Your dreams and successes are on the other side of fear. Aren't you even curious?**

Sobering realization: **The best thing about being an entrepreneur is that you have nothing limiting your success except you and your efforts. The most terrifying thing about being an entrepreneur is that you have nothing limiting your success except you and your efforts.**

That constant fear was a brick wall in my world. Now it is but a misty curtain – and my goal is to walk through it many, many times.

Change your perception, and you can change your life!

KEY takeaway: The road to success comes with a lot of twists and turns – a smooth ride at the start does not guarantee you will forfeit your share of speed bumps to come. Be prepared to re-evaluate your skills and strengths regularly so you can become the best version of yourself in life and business, no matter what!

Find more on Melissa Taylor:

www.melissataylorteam.ca

www.instagram.com/melissataylor_realestate

www.facebook.com/melissataylorkwrc/

https://www.linkedin.com/in/melissa-taylor-13a45950/?
originalSubdomain=ca

66

EMBRACE
REJECTION AS A
STEPPING STONE
TO YOUR NEXT
SUCCESS. EVERY
SETBACK IS
AN OPPORTUNITY
TO GROW.

ZIG ZIGLAR

RENATA PLECITY

🌐 renataplecity.com
📷 @renataplecity
f Renata Plecity

Renata was born and raised in the Czech Republic, the heart of Europe. From early childhood and into her teens, ski racing was a big part of her life. Skiing is still her passion to this day and you can still find her on the slopes.

After successfully earning her Master's degree in Management and Economics at Mendel University, she moved to Canada in 2001 and has called Kitchener-Waterloo her home ever since. In 2004, she launched her real estate career in partnership with RE/MAX. Fueled by hard work and a "people first" mindset, she is recognized as a top-producing agent within the organization and in the industry. She has earned RE/MAX Chairman's Club, Platinum Club, an induction into the RE/MAX Hall of Fame, and a Lifetime Achievement award.

CHAPTER 10
RENATA PLECITY

WHEN I FLEW across the ocean 23 years ago, I didn't know yet that I would stay here for 23 years, and actually, forever. When I finished University in the second half of the nineties, after the initial celebrations and parties, I finally had a diploma in my hand and naturally had to start thinking about what was next...finding a job and entering the workforce. I'm wired in such a way that when I do something, I do it properly. So, if I am selling houses, I am selling houses; if there's a party, it's a full-on party. Whether it's work, a career, or fun, it's always all-out for me.

As a fresh young 20-something, the idea that I had to start working now and begin building a career with nothing but 40 more years of the same ahead of me... that scared me a lot. It scared me to the extent that I quickly started to speculate about a way to extend that carefree student period of life a little bit longer. I had a few friends who went to the United States in the nineties, and those who returned told stories that sounded incredibly interesting and adventurous. Moreover, they brought back a bag full of dollars. At that time, the U.S. dollar was quite strong, so when they returned, they were buying beautiful cars and still had extra for traveling. That's when the idea was born. It seemed like a good plan, so I decided to give it a try, too.

I applied for a visa at the U.S. embassy, but they denied my application, and the whole wonderful idea of exploring the USA came to an end. With the benefit of hindsight, it all makes sense to me now. During the nineties, a lot of Europeans were traveling there, and at that time, America started tightening its entry requirements. Getting a visa became quite a challenge, especially for young, unmarried, childless, freshly graduated individuals like me – even though my application seemed perfect to me.

Canada bordered the United States (which I only knew from a map). Like a typical young European, I thought to myself, "It's just around the corner," which is a beautiful myth. Nothing in America nor Canada is anywhere close to being "around the corner." I applied for a visa at the Canadian embassy and hoped that Canadians would be kinder – and they were. I got a visa for six months. So, I bought a ticket to Toronto, and in the meantime, I stumbled upon an English course so I could present it to my parents as if I wasn't just going there to gallivant around but to educate myself.

The first slap in the face came after the initial few days, when you think you can speak English somewhat decently, only to realize that you really can't. The first few weeks were about getting oriented, and yes, while Canadians were indeed kinder and granted me a visa, they are also amazing at following rules to the letter. If someone in

Canada were to say that you can only drink beer with a special permit, you can bet that every Friday, they'd be at the local beer-drinking committee getting that permit sorted out. This also means that finding work "under the table" without a work permit turned out to be an utterly unachievable matter. Slap number two.

The option of returning home as a defeated person simply didn't exist for me. I'd rather die than admit defeat. So finally, my first job – a washroom cleaner. No one cared if you had education or diplomas; it was brooms, mops, vacuums, and toilet brushes. Every morning at 6:00 a.m., I endured it for eight months. As I circled around with that broom and then with a toilet brush, I was brewing a plan in my head for what was next. After eight months, I managed to climb the career ladder and got a job as a wait-ress in a private golf club – a bit of an upgrade. There were plenty of wealthy people there, and the tips were good, so the money was fairly decent.

There were a few regulars who looked incredibly success-ful, and their conversations sounded so alluring... "A million-dollar house here, a contract to be signed tomor-row, commissions..." I wondered what this group of people did for a living. From behind the bar, it sounded very lucrative and luxurious. I was very intrigued and curious. So, one day, I struck up a conversation, and lo and behold, they were real estate agents. And that's more or less where my real estate journey began. I applied to a real estate college and completed it in 18 months.

It can be done faster, but I was working at that bar deliv-ering beer to pay rent and remember, my English wasn't that strong, so studying through real estate school was quite challenging. I vividly recall my very first day in school, where I sat from 9:00 a.m. until 4:30 p.m. During that entire time, I only understood about 45 minutes of what the teacher was talking about. Essentially, my study method involved constantly looking up every second to third word in Webster's dictionary and attempting to piece together the meaning of the text.

So for me, it took a year and a half.

Now I had the paper. What's next? In the last few weeks, I had been discussing with my classmates about where each of us would go to work, and which company to sell for. Some of them already had meetings with various office owners at that time, comparing conditions, prices, advantages, and so on. While I didn't have a clear plan on how to start, I knew where and with which company I wanted to begin. I had no experience and minimal contacts. I have an accent, and my English was better but still not perfect. At that time, in the city where I operated, RE/MAX had a big share of the market, so my choice was absolutely clear.

During the first two years, I was like an energetic squirrel – making cold calls persistently. I was sitting in the office for three to four hours every day, calling, calling, calling. Door-knocking was also a regular activity two or three times a week, along with distributing flyers and hosting open houses. Of course, from these activities, I managed to generate sales, but it was intense work – lots of hours, early mornings, late evenings, Fridays, holidays, weekends – it was all about working, working, working.

One of the activities that was crucial and very successful for me was hosting open houses. It was a fantastic way to initiate contact with potential customers. For the first two or three years, I did open houses almost every weekend. As I met and talked to people, there was one thing that surprised me greatly and kept happening repeatedly. A potential customer would come to an open house, and in the course of our conversation, I would ask them if they had a real estate agent they were working with, or who they would contact if they needed help.

Most people would answer me with "No, we don't..." and the conversation would go like this:

"Do you own or are you considering buying your first property?"

"We do own one, for 10 years now, but we'd like something bigger."

"When you bought your property 10 years ago, did you buy it privately or did a real estate agent help you?"

"We had an agent but I think his name was Mike but I don't remember his last name, he was really nice, it was a pleasant collaboration."

"And if you decide to move, will you contact Mike?"

"Well, we haven't heard from him since then. I actually don't even know if he still works in real estate."

It was a very shocking revelation for me that people who came to viewings, even though they had previous experience with a real estate agent, the agent never reached out again after the transaction was completed. It felt almost like a crime to me. I had to make a real effort to acquire a client, and when we went through the whole process together, and the client was satisfied, I felt happy that everything had worked out. Why would I let them go? It was entirely evident that clients would like to return to the real estate agent and even recommend them because they had a positive experience. But since then, they haven't heard from them.

For me, it was such an "Aha!" moment when I first felt that there must be a way to stay in touch with former clients.

I made myself a promise that I would never allow a client to not know my name or to be unsure of if I'm still in the business or not – even if ten years passed – because they might require the services of a real estate agent again, or recommend me to others.

So, that was the very beginning of my vision that I wanted to work with returning customers or with customers who come through referrals.

I had been in the business for about two and a half years, and basically, I lived and breathed real estate. Everything else took a back seat. Friends faded into the background, and from morning to evening, Fridays and Saturdays, holidays, it was always just real estate, real estate, real estate, giving it my all at full throttle, 150%.

When there was a birthday party somewhere, I usually arrived late or had to leave in the middle to go deal with something or someone, or at least I was somewhere outside or in the bathroom dealing with something on the phone. That was my life for two and a half years. Working every day like this, I started to become terribly tired, and I began to feel like a squeezed lemon. While I was giving it my all, I was selling and making deals happen, and money was being made, but I was actually at the beginning of understanding people who talk about burnout syndrome, and it became clear to me that this level of dedication couldn't be sustained and endured in the long run.

Gradually, I created a system through which I work exclusively with referral/repeat clients. In 2008, I embarked on a plan that aimed at regularly acquiring referral business. Over time, I expanded the database, added activities for individual contacts, and worked toward clients being recruited solely based on referrals. However, it took another two years for things to start moving.

I began to feel unhappy because nothing was happening, and clients were essentially not coming through referrals. I admit, it was a frustrating period for me. There were days when I wanted to give up and find another way, to re-evaluate the established plan. However, within two months, it suddenly turned around. Previously unknown clients started reaching out, precisely on recommendations. That was a significant boost for me to stick to the plan and continue with the established activities.

Thanks to the referral business, my work began to change. It became more enjoyable and suddenly seemed easier to me. People from referrals knew my rules and didn't negotiate them. They were informed and, more or less, approached me with respect and trust from the beginning.

Why is working with referrals my main focus? Clients who come through recommendations already know something about me and trust me. It's much more pleasant and straightforward. Clients who recommend me set the stage for me. I don't have to negotiate commissions. And clients referred by others respect my time more.

This business model is not only financially savvy but also budget-friendly. There's no need for grandiose marketing campaigns, which translates to no hefty marketing budget. As a frugal Euro-immigrant, I'm all in for that!

The foundation of it all is a perfectly organized database! The database must be absolutely flawless, well-organized, and structured, and you must constantly update it. It's a fluid matter; you have to nurture it and keep it in perfect order. It's an endless project. Thanks to learning how to perfectly understand my database and manage it, I have been achieving very consistent results in recent years, allowing me to achieve the desired balance between free time and work.

My database is divided into several categories, each with its own significance, and each category also determines how much attention a contact requires. Thanks to the database, I have a perfect overview of my surroundings. I know who has potential, who needs care, and with whom it's not necessary to waste time. Occasionally, someone comes on their own, so-called "walk-ins." But it happens rarely. These are clients I consider a "bonus." It's nice when it happens, but I don't always count on it in my production plan. I make my living from clients who come based on referrals.

Working with referrals requires commitment, discipline, and consistency. You need to have a plan and stick to it. It will take time, and it might be challenging, but over the years, it can transform your life.

The most important thing is to start, equally important is to continue, and above all, do not deviate, do not waver, and do not give up.

I wish you the best of luck.

KEY takeaway: Decide on your vision, create a strategic plan, and stick to it. If you focus on building relationships, over time this will lead to more fun and fulfilling work with less stress and a lot more balance between work and personal life. You only live once!

Find more on Renata Plecity:

www.renataplecity.com

www.instagram.com/renataplecity

www.facebook.com/renata.plecity

SAM
ABDALLAH

🌐 affluencergroup.com
📷 @samabdallah_kw

Sam is a passionate business owner who embraces his core values of contribution, value, and growth. Sam is always striving to be a better version of himself each day, to learn, and to apply something new. He has been teaching at market centers and is part of the leadership council in the Keller Williams Brokerage with his own team as a listing specialist in Kitchener Waterloo, serving a 45-minute radius of the area.

Sam's superpowers are connecting to people and finding value in relationships. He has a passion for books and learning about marketing so he can create a message that matches the market.

CHAPTER 11
SAM ABDALLAH

ALL RIGHT, it's me. Not the sole author, but someone with a story that can inspire. I'm a figure in the Real Estate Industry who has witnessed the positive impact of this business. It has shaped my life and has helped me to discover my true values. I strive each day to live them to the fullest, extending grace and gratitude wherever I can. During one of my recent contemplative walks, I had some profound reflections, and I'd like to share them with you. These insights hold significance, and I'll elaborate on them to a certain extent. Some sayings deeply resonate with me, and I trust they'll resonate with you as well.

Life is fundamentally about the person you evolve and grow into. This business continually shapes you, even when you don't realize it, requiring you to achieve higher results and serve more people. There are two types of work. Work that's working for you or working on you, raising your beliefs, identity allowing you to achieve whatever it is your here for and your purpose. The wonderful thing about real estate is that it's a continuous growth journey. When you look at all 'circles' of your life, health, financial, relationships, career, personal, it causes you to reflect, grow and continuously re-evaluate and iterate learning from failures and re-defining your purpose. I do my best to teach from real life business and not just something I learned from a book yesterday. This aligns with the law of service – the act of giving without expecting, where education builds connections, trust begets business, and referrals flow organically. There's also the principle of detachment; when you free yourself from fixating on specific outcomes, you open the door to attracting more people and favourable circumstances into your life. I also believe that when you have a giving heart and truly desire to contribute, you make other's lives better and real estate is a natural byproduct of those strong relationships built.

As realtors, we are always finding a balance between increasing our knowledge of marketing, sales, solving problems for others and helping others achieve their goals while we grow our business. True generosity stems from the heart of a genuine servant, without expecting anything in return. For instance, in my passion for the growth minded realtors and expanding on my gifts I feel I have a need to serve, I came up with the "350 formula". This is not mere self promotion, just an idea or example how one must listen to their desires, need to contribute and bring their own magic to the marketplace. This revolutionary way to help Realtors organize their database to increase conversion truly came from learning the biggest needs in the Realtor community, filling a gap and allowing our services as a bridge to help solve a problem for our client (in this case, Realtors). It's an idea that has ignited my inspiration and is firmly planted on my ever-growing list of innovative concepts. In other words, it is on a sticky note with lots of other 'to action' in future ideas:).

Once your systems are optimized and you've attained a considerable level of proficiency, it's prudent to consider your next hire. Engage as a diligent student of the market; in moments of market downturns for others, seek out opportunities. For instance, if investors are grappling, contemplate shifting your focus toward sellers who could benefit from your expertise during their renewal phase. Looking for the gift in every hardship. I always see how we can turn them into opportunities. For instance, during the recent downturn of the market, we focused on how to improve our messaging, social media presence, AB testing and going deeper with our relationships. It proved to help us overcome a challenging year. The point here is that old adage "don't wish it were easier, wish you were better" This statement is so true. In showing up each day, over-coming challenges, turning them into opportunities, getting better each day, focusing on 3 the needle movers that day, you can truly create magic in your marketplace. I truly feel that clients, prospects and everyone notices although, ironically, you do this for yourself. Wealth and business growth truly is a spiritual journey.

Your capacity to connect hinges on the emotional trust you deposit into your relationships. This trust serves as a bridge, ensuring they'll be inclined to answer your call. Establishing a connection paves the way for meaningful conversations, which, in turn, fill the gaps and culminate in successful sales.

To be your authentic self, it's crucial to heal your inner child and present yourself spiritually. The energy you radiate in the workplace doesn't go unnoticed by your customers and clients. Immerse yourself deeply in whatever you pursue – commit to perfecting your craft and your dialogues. Avoid chasing the next shiny object; instead, embark on an "idea fast." Implement, allocate time for testing these ideas, and iterate. Mastery wields a magnetic energy, attracting those who seek to be served by you. Any hesitancy in making calls often stems from a lack of understanding your audience and articulating the right message that resonates with them.

Remember the "Problem, Agitate, Solution" approach. Discover your client's true problem (it's about what they need, not what you do), understand how it affects them emotionally, and offer a solution that alleviates their pain. The greater the problem you solve, the more substantial your income – an insight beautifully encapsulated by Robin Sharma: your income is directly proportional to your impact.

Personal touches never fail to make a lasting impression. Have faith, and instil trust. How many Realtors do you know who take the time to call on birthdays?

Remember, it's not a lead problem, but rather a connection problem. There's no reason why you can't convert unfamiliar leads into fervent supporters who trust and champion your endeavours.

In real estate education, the conventional sequence seems inverted. There's a plethora of tactical training on procedures that are prone to obsolescence and processes that are ever-evolving. However, the most pivotal factor lies in identifying your values early on. These values not only serve as your compass in perceiving the world but also necessitate a genuine affection for personal development. A servant's heart and a spirit of contribution form the nucleus of a referral-based business. While your clients may not consciously acknowledge it, they can intuitively discern if your motives are solely self-serving. To simplify, think about your clients problems more than you do and how you can solve them, be easy for people to find you and you will have an incredible real estate career!

Amidst the abundance of valuable dialogues, training programs, and tools available, I won't delve into exhaustive detail. What I will emphasize is this: sales isn't something you do "to" someone; it's something you do "for" someone. We kick off with a fundamental question for our clients: "What are you hoping to achieve?" By delving into their needs and becoming passionately engrossed in resolving their challenges, we position ourselves for success – regardless of market conditions.

In any market, opportunities invariably exist. In a climate where many businesses experienced a 70% decline, we are on track to surpass last year's performance. Why, you may wonder? It's straightforward. Always continue growing and learning, taking action, iterating testing and re-learning. I always ask myself "what golden nugget will you take from training?"

I remember back in 2016, I went on my first solo trip (believe it or not). Growing up in a fairly limited-thinking household, being labeled was a big deal for me. I was labeled as someone who had difficulty traveling alone, as if I wasn't "capable" or labeled with "anxiety."

Later, I realized that this was all a result of programming and environment (I digress), but there's a point here. Real estate enabled my self-growth and inner journey to over-come. Boarding that plane, using the techniques I learned from NLP (neuro-linguistic programming), and envi-sioning an incredibly enjoyable outcome – for most, it was just a landing. For me, it was an epic moment of growth. I did it. I shattered every limiting belief in the "book." I got to rewrite my story, tear out the pages, and craft a new narrative and ending, while also rephrasing those limiting beliefs into liberating truths.

During that trip, I embarked on a journey of growth. They say your brain's reticular activating system searches for what you're focusing on. For me, it was all about growth and seizing opportunities. I remember feeling called, in spiritual terms, to book a consultation with a Mega Agent Production Systems (coaching company) "MAPS"coach at the time. I did it boldly. Even without having the money to fully believe in myself, I practically embodied the princi-ples of a good mentor, David Nagle, from *The Science of Getting Rich* by Wallace Wattles. I was truly "acting as if." I booked the better flights, even if I wasn't quite able to afford them yet. I recognized that everything I do shapes my subconscious mind, either towards scarcity or abundance.

When I started in real estate, I realized I had undergone significant growth over those three years, and even more from 2018 until now! Quickly rewinding, it's important to note one thing: You're guided to increase your level of awareness to tackle bigger and bigger problems. The more you honour yourself (contribution and integrity are among my core values), the more confidence, belief, and trust I have in myself. Whether it's making my morning calls or committing to call my seller on Wednesday and dig for feedback, I believe we all yearn for that sense of contribution and meaning in our work. Money is simply a reflection of the value we bring to the marketplace.

Returning to "acting as if" – remember your defining moment? That moment when you realized you were living in a program, a pattern – and you began seeking resources and other things to help you break free? Speaking of programming, Myron Golden talks about the "poverty programming trap." Not to get too religious here, but he speaks about the notion that "money is evil" and how superheroes subconsciously indoctrinate our children to act in accordance. After all, Aaron Doughty, a spiritual mentor of mine a few years back, said, "If you keep people at a lower level of vibration or consciousness, you can control them."

I mention this programming trap because I recall my wife placing the book "The Secret" on DVD in my car at the time, and my initial negative thoughts. I could tell my brain's subconscious patterns were in a negative state in 2015. Yet, I realized I had started to program myself for success. This is where I owe a tremendous debt to the love of my life, Patricia. After crying for multiple days when I first entered real estate, leaving my "secure" job at the call centre – which did equip me with phone skills – granted, it was a huge leap. We both left our jobs, relying on her maternity leave income. I had it on my mirror. It's true what Napoleon Hill says: "With repetition, you can become programmed to believe anything." I would look at that number and not realize it was programming me for success.

Let's be clear, it didn't magically bring about the number. However, it led me to the people, circumstances, and events that made it happen. As it turned out, I joined a successful team that helped me learn a lot about real estate, apply my sales skills, and develop discipline. I sold 24 homes in my first year, and my Gross Commissions Income number was pretty much the number in that mirror. Regardless of any market, opportunities abound. Even if your market seems "down" with 1800 agents and 9000 transactions, there's still ample potential to build a thriving career, achieving your goal of selling 40 homes, 50 homes, or even more.

Embarking on a spiritual journey, I delved into Joe Dispenza's wisdom on how our thoughts and experiences wire together. Through meditation and mental pruning, I learned to discern unhelpful thoughts and release them. My spiritual path led me to discover timeline therapy, a fascinating process. I courageously ventured into my past, forgiving my narcissistic father, and embracing love and forgiveness for my family. This allowed me to gracefully release that chapter of my life, suffused with gratitude and well-wishes.

Gratefulness and forgiveness became my guiding lights, even in moments of distance. As Gabrielle Bernstein aptly puts it, faith transcends fear, and I've come to trust in a higher power that guides my path. Obstacles have transformed into valuable lessons, for which I am eternally thankful. Each day, I'm surrounded by people, places, experiences, and energies that enrich my life, giving true meaning and purpose to my work. This continuous process honed my skills, nurtured healthy self-esteem, and bolstered my confidence to not only believe in myself but also to support others in achieving their goals.

I eagerly anticipate the adventures life has in store for me. I hold a steadfast belief that when you're aligned with your purpose, things flow effortlessly. There's no need for resistance. Life's currents carry you forward, bringing people, places, and circumstances that align with your journey. So, take that next step with confidence. Don't fret about perfection. Simply start, and let progress be your guide. Remember, "done" always trumps "perfect."

KEY takeaway: Working on yourself is quite possibly the best thing you can do for your business. Become the person who is always *becoming* a better version.

Find more on Sam Abdallah:

www.affluenceregroup.com

www.instagram.com/samabdallah_kw

TERRI HASTINGS

🌐 terrihastings.ca
🌐 worldclasswaterfront.ca

With 18 years of experience, Terri Hastings is a prominent figure in the real estate industry, excelling not only as a Realtor® but also as an investor, author, guest speaker, and presenter. As the leader of The Terri Hastings Real Estate Group, she has consistently earned accolades, both individually and as the top group in her brokerage for several years.

Terri's 25-year sales journey spans diverse industries and geographical locations, beginning at the age of 18 when she purchased her first home and ignited her passion for real estate. With a diverse portfolio including residential properties, an island, and commercial real estate, Terri remains committed to helping clients achieve their real estate goals by continuously seeking new opportunities in the ever-evolving landscape of the industry.

CHAPTER 12
TERRI HASTINGS

THE PATH to becoming a Realtor® and stepping into the dynamic world of real estate is an ambition shared by many. Eighteen years ago, I was one of those aspiring professionals who embarked on this exciting yet challenging journey. Obtaining a real estate license is a crucial first step, but it's essential to acknowledge that this path is marked by significant hurdles, and the statistics paint a sobering picture. Approximately 87% of Realtors® face difficulties and struggles within their initial 2-3 years in the industry. I knew that I didn't want to be just another statistic, and my determination set me on a unique course.

My journey commenced with rigorous studying and the pursuit of a real estate license. Like many others, I faced exam failures along the way. However, these setbacks are an all-too-common part of the journey. The truth is, succeeding in real estate is far from guaranteed. The statistics reveal that the majority of newcomers in the field struggle during their first few years. This fact didn't deter me; instead, it fueled my determination.

Upon obtaining my real estate license, I took the next step by joining a brokerage. This marked the beginning of my exciting journey as a Realtor®. I was granted an office, and the initial thrill of setting up my own real estate business was palpable. However, there was a stark reality I had to face. Despite being equipped with the necessary credentials and a designated workspace, the road ahead was far from easy. Every day I walked into the office, but every day, I was met with a daunting lack of business prospects.

As the days turned into weeks and months, I couldn't help but wonder – how do I build a successful real estate business? Where were the clients and prospects I had envisioned? I understood that waiting for business to come to me was not a viable strategy. It was time to seek answers, to learn the ropes of this challenging industry. I approached my brokerage, hoping to find guidance and support. Instead, I was directed to training videos and left to navigate the complexities of real estate on my own. This isolation was not unique, as many newcomers in the field find themselves in a similar predicament. Additionally, seeking assistance from my fellow Realtors® within the brokerage proved to be a fruitless endeavour, as they were reluctant to share their own successful strategies.

The initial period in the real estate business can be a stark and lonely place. It's an environment where you're left to sink or swim, with little guidance or support. It was during this challenging phase that I discovered the importance of open houses. I realized that without any property listings of my own, this strategy offered a glimmer of hope. To get started, I approached Realtors® within my brokerage who had listings and asked for the opportunity to host open houses for them. The response from my colleagues was mixed; only a few agreed, and among them was the owner of the brokerage. This marked a significant turning point in my journey.

Despite this initial breakthrough, my journey was far from smooth sailing. Hosting open houses was a valuable experience, allowing me to connect with potential buyers. However, it wasn't without its challenges. Some of the prospective buyers I encountered during open houses were not genuinely interested in making a purchase. Their lack of commitment and indecision often resulted in wasted time and effort. This was a valuable lesson in the perils of lead generation in the real estate industry.

Earning the trust and respect of clients is a pivotal aspect of success in the real estate business. I recognized that to survive in this highly competitive industry, I couldn't simply rely on open houses or hope that clients would come my way. I needed to take a more proactive approach. I began attending events and positioning myself in places where I believed potential clients frequented. The goal was to make my presence known, be of help, and become a trusted resource in their real estate journey. However, it was an incredibly time-consuming way to become known, and it didn't come without its challenges.

Realizing the limitations of my initial approach, I knew I had to find a more effective way to generate leads and secure clients. I couldn't rely solely on in-person interactions and random encounters. As a newcomer with limited resources, I couldn't compete with the big producers who could pour money into marketing. The understanding that I needed a robust lead generation strategy was crucial. The lesson was clear; without the ability to effectively generate leads, I risked falling into the 87% of Realtors® who don't make it in their first 2-3 years in the business.

The realization that I needed a more systematic approach to my real estate business began to take root. To streamline and optimize my operations, I started with an Administrative Assistant. This marked the birth of a systematic approach, with clearly defined tasks that my assistant would handle. The goal was to free up my time, allowing me to focus on the critical aspects of growing my business, making more money, and finding some much-needed free time.

The introduction of an Administrative Assistant was a significant step forward, but I didn't stop there. I realized that to truly succeed and thrive in the real estate business, I needed systems for everything. Whether it was lead generation, managing deal paperwork, or handling office procedures, I recognized the need for structured processes and well-defined systems to ensure efficiency and consistency.

As I continued to develop and implement systems, my fellow Realtors® and even the brokerage owner began to take notice. They saw the positive impact these systems were having on my business, and they expressed interest in replicating my approach. I was more than willing to share the overarching concepts and strategies, but I held on to the intricacies of the "how" for myself. This protective mindset was a characteristic of traditional brokerages, and I knew that if I wanted to grow further, I needed to break free from it. The future called for a brokerage that supported our goals and offered a culture of collaboration and growth.

Amidst this period of growth and transition, an unexpected turn of events took place. My Administrative Assistant's husband's job took them out of the area, leading to her departure. Simultaneously, a colleague and friend who had been struggling in the real estate business faced severe financial difficulties, putting her home at risk. To my surprise, the brokerage decided to take away her office space and instructed her to work from home. This raised fundamental questions about the industry and how it handled challenges.

Amid this adversity, I saw an opportunity. I believed in my struggling colleague's potential and offered her a full-time position as an Administrative Assistant with a guaranteed salary. The plan was to retrain her, equipping her with the skills and knowledge needed to excel in the real estate business. After a year, she would have the choice to transition into a full-time sales role, and this would mean the end of her salary. It was a leap of faith, but it turned out to be a remarkable success story. She not only redeemed herself but also achieved a six-figure income in that year. Tragically, she later succumbed to a severe illness, but she departed knowing her true worth as a successful Realtor®.

In the year of transformation, I created a comprehensive marketing, lead generation, and training system. This system not only guided my colleague to success but also propelled my business to a level where I had more clients than I could handle. With the business booming, I continued to introduce more systems to enhance efficiency and productivity. Recognizing the need for specialized roles, I brought a professional photographer/videographer on board. This addition to our team meant we no longer had to rely on external companies with lengthy turn-around times to capture property listings. This move expedited the marketing of our properties and enhanced our overall service.

At this point, our team consisted of an Administrative/Marketing Assistant, a photographer, and me. While our systems continued to bring in business, managing both clients and administrative responsibilities became increasingly challenging. Long hours remained a constant in my daily routine.

The mounting workload and the need for a more sustainable way of doing business led to a crucial realization. I understood that I could not do it all on my own. It was time to consider expanding by bringing other Realtors® onto the team. In exchange for covering their fees, marketing, training, coaching, mentoring, and granting them access to my systems, I would provide them with a share of the business.

With the recruitment of our first team member, our business saw substantial growth. In just three years, we expanded to a team of ten full-time Realtors®. Simultaneously, the demands on the Administrative/Marketing role grew to the point where it made sense to split it into two full-time positions to accommodate our growth. The journey of leading a real estate team brought with it a unique set of challenges. These challenges are too numerous to list here and deserve their own chapter for detailed exploration. However, the rewards of helping others succeed in the industry are a source of immense satisfaction for the team leader.

The real estate business offers numerous rewards, both personal and professional. The most gratifying moment is seeing a big smile on the face of a satisfied buyer or seller. It's a reminder that all of the challenges, struggles, and hard work are worthwhile, and they fuel our passion to continue in this exciting and dynamic industry.

KEY takeaway: Finding business success will come much quicker when the right people are in the right places on your team. Don't be afraid to rise by pulling others up with you.

Find more on Terri Hastings:

www.terihastings.ca

www.worldclasswaterfront.ca

TINA KOTHARI

shrinerealty.ca
@tinakrealtor
@tinakothari2385
Tina K Realtor
@tkrealtor1

As a Broker of Record, Tina is passionate about connecting and working with people to help them make the right decisions. Her team at Shrine Realty Brokerage Ltd. in London is a thriving business that has seen fast success. She has committed herself to working in the client's best interest and to providing them with outstanding service in the buying and selling of their real estate property.

In a short period, she has enhanced her portfolio and provided extensive services to all her clients involved in both Residential and Commercial purchase and sale. Over the years, Tina has enhanced her skills in multiple areas including marketing, branding, communication, negotiation, and customer service.

CHAPTER 13
TINA KOTHARI

JUST IMAGINE a 10-year-old girl who knew very little about the business world, but had a dream to be a successful entrepreneur. Becoming a successful entrepreneur is challenging but is an absolutely rewarding journey.

I was born in Ahmedabad, a city in Gujarat, India. It's a country full of excitement, culture, colours, music, dance, festivals, and overall, it's very social. After pursuing my education, and receiving my Bachelor of Commerce and Diploma in Multimedia, I started working in the multi-media field, as well as started a freelance website design, animation, and graphics business at the young age of 22. My life was full of energy, friends, family, a good career, and everything else that one could ask for.

After my marriage, I migrated to London, Ontario, Canada. I still remember the day I landed, with two suit-cases and all of my dreams to conquer the new world. The willingness to take risks and face the unknown is often a crucial factor in personal growth and success. Navigating a new country's systems, culture, and job market often requires continuous learning and self-improvement.

With English being my second language, I had challenges communicating with the locals. Being a go-getter and having an outgoing personality, staying at home was not a choice for me. Within a few weeks, I managed to have a successful interview and a job offer at an outbound call centre, where I had to sell products over the phone. Although perhaps a small step towards selling, it was a big step for me to come out of my comfort zone.

My commitment to working hard to improve my accent, adapt to a new environment, and excel in the tasks I had been given was truly challenging. It reflected my determination, resilience, and dedication to achieving my goals. In just a few weeks, I was able to meet my target and managed to earn a bonus at my job. What I learned was that a positive mindset can have a significant impact on your overall well-being and personal growth. Small achievements can indeed boost your confidence and provide a sense of accomplishment. The biggest lesson coming out of that job was that lifelong learners are better equipped to navigate change and thrive in evolving environments. Every experience, whether positive or challenging, can offer valuable lessons.

After a few months, I was offered a position at a well-known insurance company in London, Ontario for a data entry position. From there, I progressed very well in different sectors and job scales for eight years. Although the job was comfortable and safe, this was not enough for me. It was clear that my entrepreneurial spirit was alive and well, even in the face of frustration. Before I made any changes, the universe had a better plan for me. Due to some confidential changes at the company, I lost the job, but setbacks can often lead to new opportunities. The true belief that certain events or experiences in life are guided by a higher power or a greater plan is something you don't realize until you experience it.

After browsing a few options, I decided to make a change in my career and progressed towards the journey as a Realtor®. I started studying when my first daughter was four, and I was pregnant with my second child. Although it was challenging, my mind was set to continue my education even though I had a newborn baby in my arms. The real challenge was to manage my career and maintain a balanced family life with two young children. The vision was clear, and I felt as though I was headed in the right direction towards my entrepreneurship dreams.

To become a successful Realtor®, there are many qualities that you must possess: having a strong work ethic, a positive attitude, clear communication, negotiation skills, marketing skills, and a genuine passion for what you do. When you're hungry for work, you're motivated to give your best effort and to continually improve your skills. Offering top-notch service to clients and customers is a cornerstone of building a successful business. The fact is, when you prioritize quality and customer satisfaction, you not only earn loyalty but also attract new opportunities through referrals. Going above and beyond what is expected, can make a significant difference in your professional journey.

Apart from the above skills, networking is very important for the business. Developing a professional relationship with your fellow Realtors®, or entrepreneurs from different fields, can always help you grow. More often than not, you will learn something new from successful people which can help you to grow. If you want to be successful then you need to associate yourself with like-minded people. Surrounding yourself with like-minded people who share your goals and ambitions is motivating and inspiring. It can create a supportive environment that encourages you to strive for success. Building a strong network can provide access to resources and connections that you might not have had otherwise. Participate in industry events, conferences, and local business meetups to meet potential contacts. Utilize social media platforms like LinkedIn, Instagram, Facebook, etc. to connect with professionals in your field and join industry-related groups. It is crucial to manage your time and energy wisely. Focus your networking efforts on those relationships that have the most potential for mutual benefit. Positive and motivated individuals can help boost your energy and drive, while negative influences can drain your motivation. These are all things that I did, and they greatly contributed to my success. That being said, the journey to get from "Real Estate Sales Representative" to "Broker of Record" was difficult, especially in this demanding and challenging field.

It is always tough to break the ice but once you do, the ride goes on. I still remember my first real estate deal, where a few of my showings were accompanied by my newborn baby girl in her car seat. The negotiation went back and forth for almost two months. In between, we almost lost the deal, but strong negotiation, consistency, and persistence helped me to make a sale for a purchase worth over a million dollars for my clients. It was a great kick start for a beginner. What I learned during that first negotiation is that empathy is a vital skill in real estate. Put yourself in your client's shoes to understand their emotions and concerns. Every client is unique, and their needs and preferences vary. You must tailor your services to meet their specific requirements and offer personalized recommendations and solutions based on their goals.

After having a successful career path as a full-time Realtor®, followed by a Broker license, I took a step ahead toward a leadership role as a "Broker of Record" and launched "Shrine Realty Brokerage Ltd." in February of 2022. It was the beginning of endless possibilities.

As a broker of record, managing director, and owner-operator of Shrine Realty Brokerage Ltd, I have evolved and developed various skills essential for the growth and success of my business. It is important to maintain and nurture these skills as you progress in your career, as continuously seeking ways to improve and grow, both professionally and personally, can lead to even greater accomplishments in the future.

I always tell my new agents that building a successful business takes time. Be patient with yourself and the process. It is a journey that often requires time, dedication, and perseverance, and I like to stress the importance of learning and adapting. The business landscape is constantly evolving, and staying up to date with industry trends, customer preferences, and new technologies is crucial. There will be challenges and setbacks along the way. I emphasize the need to stay resilient and not be discouraged by failures as each setback can provide valuable lessons for future success.

Real estate is indeed a service industry, and the way you interact with and understand your client's needs is crucial for success in this field. Buying or selling a home can be a highly emotional process and showing empathy can build trust and rapport. One should maintain a high level of professionalism in all of your interactions. Dress appropriately, be punctual for appointments, and conduct yourself with integrity and honesty. Always treat your client the way you want to be treated.

A very rewarding aspect of this profession is making a positive impact on people's lives and helping them achieve their financial goals. The sense of accomplishment and satisfaction that comes from helping others achieve financial strength and stability can be immensely fulfilling. Knowing that you've played a part in their success is a powerful motivator. The role of a Realtor® goes beyond just facilitating property transactions; it involves improving the financial well-being and quality of life for clients. The passion for helping people and making a positive impact in their lives is a testament to the value I bring to my profession.

At Shrine Realty Brokerage Ltd. we provide full services to our clients starting from searching for a property to offering our extensive legal team – and everything in between – including but not limited to negotiating, clear communication, a home inspector, photographer, home renovation contractor, movers, home stager, mortgage specialist, and more.

Real estate transactions can be some of the most significant financial decisions in a person's life. Treating people with respect, understanding their needs, and providing exceptional service not only helps you succeed in the industry but also ensures that your clients have a positive and stress-free experience.

KEY takeaway: Building a Real Estate Business is a journey that requires dedication, perseverance, and a willingness to learn and adapt. Life events can indeed present unexpected opportunities, and it's up to you to seize them and use them to your advantage. Challenges are inevitable, but they also present opportunities for growth and innovation.

Find more on Tina Kothari:

www.shrinerealty.ca

www.tiktok.com/@tkrealtor1

www.youtube.com/@tinakothari2385

www.instagram.com/tinakrealtor

www.facebook.com/tinakrealtor

CONCLUSION

RUNNING a business is no walk in the park. As an entrepreneur, you're regularly faced with challenges and roadblocks that you have no choice but to conquer — often without a clear path forward and no map to help you make a decision.

While I am not a real estate agent, I *am* a business owner. Through reading these deeply personal first-hand accounts of what it takes to grow a successful real estate business, I have realized there are many consistent key takeaways we can absorb about entrepreneurship in general through these author's stories:

1. **There is no *one* way to run a successful real estate business.** Just like when you decide to plan a road trip with your family, there are always multiple routes and paths to your destination. Success is not one-size-fits-all, and each these authors have proved this is true by sharing their journeys. Your path will be inherently unique, and that's incredibly powerful.

2. **Mentorship is your biggest asset**. Nearly every author touched on the importance of finding a person or a team of people you trust who are just a few steps ahead of you on this journey. Finding people you can connect and learn from is such an essential piece of any entrepreneurship journey. You don't need to reinvent the wheel in order to find your own success — lean into leadership from mentors, and then prepare to turn around and reach for the hand of the next agent who craves support. We're all in this together!

3. **Build a growth mindset.** Some chapters pointed directly to this concept (including referencing work by Carol Dweck), while others alluded more subjectively to the idea of fostering a mindset focused on learning for the purpose of becoming a better agent and business owner. Either way, a key theme throughout this book is to find ways to improve and grow through keeping an open, positive, growth-focused mindset. This is a solid piece of advice in both life and business. "A negative mind will never give you a positive life." —*Ziad K. Abdelnour*

4. **We're better together.** *This book is a perfect example of collaboration at its finest.* If two heads are better than one, multiple heads are better than two. Finding a circle of people who can help you along your journey is just as essential as finding a personal mentor. Finding connection alongside likeminded people will always generate a more comprehensive view of the topic at hand. In this book, you get to experience a multitude of different perspectives on business success — not just one single view. Similarly, by finding a group of likeminded business colleagues to connect with, you will elevate your own perspectives on success in business...*and in life.*

The insights and learnings shared throughout this book have been powerful to consider. This is true for any collaborative book project I have produced since founding LeadHer Publishing in 2018.

If you are an aspiring real estate agent, I hope you found valuable advice and suggestions for starting or growing your own business in the industry. If you resonated with author or story in particular, I highly encourage you to reach out and connect with that person directly via the provided links at the end of each chapter.

Thank you for being a part of this book and for taking into consideration the perspectives of this unique and diverse team of authors.

Courtney St Croix

Founder, LeadHer Publishing

To find out more about LeadHer Publishing, visit www.leadherpublishing.com or go to www.instagram.com/leadherpublishing, www.tiktok.com/@leadherpublishing or www.youtube.com/@leadherpublishing

66

THE ONLY LIMIT TO OUR REALIZATION OF TOMORROW WILL BE OUR DOUBTS OF TODAY.

FRANKLIN D. ROOSEVELT

ABOUT THE LEAD AUTHOR

Because she was *Raised with Real Estate*™ her entire life, Jessica Hastings-Lesperance has had a front row seat to some of the top-producing Realtors® in the country. She is Co-Owner, Marketing Visionary, Director of Operations and Realtor® at the Terri Hastings Real Estate Group/Keller Williams Realty Centres, one of the top producing Keller Williams teams in all of Canada.

Jessica is an inspiring entrepreneur, real estate investor, coach, speaker, and published author. She has been featured on major media outlets including podcasts and real estate TV talk shows and has been published in various magazines. Recently, she was recognized as one of Canada's Top Fitness Instructors for 2023 by Impact Magazine. Jessica is extremely passionate about helping her community and continues to have a positive impact by supporting local initiatives including homeless shelters, hospitals and mental health awareness campaigns. She continues to inspire others and celebrate change.

Find out more:

www.jessicahastingslesperance.ca

"

> # SUCCESS IS NOT THE RESULT OF SPONTANEOUS COMBUSTION. YOU MUST SET YOURSELF ON FIRE.
>
> ARNOLD H. GLASOW

leadher
PUBLISHING

**PUBLISHED IN PARTNERSHIP
WITH LEADHER PUBLISHING**

Find out more at
leadherpublishing.com